T0249671

Computation and Storage in the Cloud

Computation and Storage in the Cloud
Understanding the Trade-Offs

Dong Yuan and Yun Yang

Centre for Computing and Engineering Software Systems,
Faculty of Information and Communication Technologies,
Swinburne University of Technology,
Hawthorn, Melbourne, Australia

Jinjun Chen

Centre for Innovation in IT Services and Applications,
Faculty of Engineering and Information Technology,
University of Technology,
Sydney, Australia

ELSEVIER

AMSTERDAM • BOSTON • HEIDELBERG • LONDON • NEW YORK • OXFORD
PARIS • SAN DIEGO • SAN FRANCISCO • SINGAPORE • SYDNEY • TOKYO

Elsevier

225 Wyman Street, Waltham, MA 02451, USA

32 Jamestown Road, London NW1 7BY

First edition 2013

Copyright © 2013 Elsevier Inc. All rights reserved

No part of this publication may be reproduced or transmitted in any form or by any means, electronic or mechanical, including photocopying, recording, or any information storage and retrieval system, without permission in writing from the publisher. Details on how to seek permission, further information about the Publisher's permissions policies and our arrangement with organizations such as the Copyright Clearance Center and the Copyright Licensing Agency, can be found at our website: www.elsevier.com/permissions

This book and the individual contributions contained in it are protected under copyright by the Publisher (other than as may be noted herein).

Notices

Knowledge and best practice in this field are constantly changing. As new research and experience broaden our understanding, changes in research methods, professional practices, or medical treatment may become necessary.

Practitioners and researchers must always rely on their own experience and knowledge in evaluating and using any information, methods, compounds, or experiments described herein.

In using such information or methods they should be mindful of their own safety and the safety of others, including parties for whom they have a professional responsibility.

To the fullest extent of the law, neither the Publisher nor the authors, contributors, or editors, assume any liability for any injury and/or damage to persons or property as a matter of products liability, negligence or otherwise, or from any use or operation of any methods, products, instructions, or ideas contained in the material herein.

Library of Congress Cataloging-in-Publication Data
A catalog record for this book is available from the Library of Congress

British Library Cataloguing-in-Publication Data
A catalogue record for this book is available from the British Library

ISBN: 978-0-12-407767-6

For information on all Elsevier publications
visit our website at store.elsevier.com

This book has been manufactured using Print On Demand technology. Each copy is produced to order and is limited to black ink. The online version of this book will show color figures where appropriate.

Working together to grow
libraries in developing countries

www.elsevier.com | www.bookaid.org | www.sabre.org

ELSEVIER   BOOK AID
             International   Sabre Foundation

Contents

Acknowledgements

The authors are grateful for the discussions with Dr. Willem van Straten and Ms. Lina Levin from the Swinburne Centre for Astrophysics and Supercomputing regarding the pulsar searching scientific workflow. This work is supported by the Australian Research Council under Discovery Project DP110101340.

About the Authors

Dong Yuan received his PhD degree in Computer Science and Software Engineering from the Faculty of Information and Communication Technologies at Swinburne University of Technology, Melbourne, Australia in 2012. He received his Master and Bachelor degrees from the School of Computer Science and Technology, Shandong University, Jinan, China in 2008 and 2005, respectively, all in Computer Science. He is currently a postdoctoral research fellow in the Centre of Computing and Engineering Software System at Swinburne University of Technology. His research interests include data management in parallel and distributed systems, scheduling and resource management, and grid and cloud computing.

Yun Yang received a Master of Engineering degree from the University of Science and Technology of China, Hefei, China in 1987, and a PhD degree from the University of Queensland, Brisbane, Australia in 1992, all in Computer Science. He is currently a full professor in the Faculty of Information and Communication Technologies at Swinburne University of Technology, Melbourne, Australia. Prior to joining Swinburne as an associate professor in late 1999, he was a lecturer and senior lecturer at Deakin University during 1996–1999. Before that, he was a research scientist at DSTC – Cooperative Research Centre for Distributed Systems Technology – during 1993–1996. He also worked at Beihang University in China during 1987–1988. He has published about 200 papers on journals and refereed numerous conferences. His research interests include software engineering; P2P, grid and cloud computing; workflow systems; service-oriented computing; Internet computing applications; and CSCW.

 **Jinjun Chen** received his PhD degree in Computer Science and Software Engineering from Swinburne University of Technology, Melbourne, Australia in 2007. He is currently an associate professor in the Faculty of Engineering and Information Technology, University of Technology, Sydney, Australia. His research interests include scientific workflow management and applications; workflow management and applications in Web service or SOC environments; workflow management and applications in grid (service)/cloud computing environments; software verification and validation in workflow systems; QoS and resource scheduling in distributed computing systems such as cloud computing, service-oriented computing, semantics and knowledge management; and cloud computing.

Preface

Nowadays, scientific research increasingly relies on IT technologies, where large-scale and high-performance computing systems (e.g. clusters, grids and super-computers) are utilised by the communities of researchers to carry out their applications. Scientific applications are usually computation and data-intensive, where complex computation tasks take a long time for execution and the generated data sets are often terabytes or petabytes in size. Storing valuable generated application data sets can save their regeneration cost when they are reused, not to mention the waiting time caused by regeneration. However, the large size of the scientific data sets makes their storage a big challenge.

In recent years, cloud computing is emerging as the latest distributed computing paradigm which provides redundant, inexpensive and scalable resources on demand to system requirements. It offers researchers a new way to deploy computation and data-intensive applications (e.g. scientific applications) without any infrastructure investments. Large generated application data sets can be flexibly stored or deleted (and regenerated whenever needed) in the cloud, since, theoretically, unlimited storage and computation resources can be obtained from commercial cloud service providers.

With the pay-as-you-go model, the total application cost for generated data sets in the cloud depends chiefly on the method used for storing them. For example, storing all the generated application data sets in the cloud may result in a high storage cost since some data sets may be seldom used but large in size; but if we delete all the generated data sets and regenerate them every time they are needed, the computation cost may also be very high. Hence, there is a trade-off between computation and storage in the cloud. In order to reduce the overall application cost, a good strategy is to find a balance to selectively store some popular data sets and regenerate the rest when needed. This book focuses on cost-effective data sets storage of scientific applications in the cloud, which is currently a leading-edge and challenging topic. By investigating the niche issue of computation and storage trade-off, we (1) propose a new cost model for data sets storage in the cloud; (2) develop novel benchmarking approaches to find the minimum cost of storing the application data; and (3) design innovative runtime storage strategies to store the application data in the cloud.

We start with introducing a motivating example from astrophysics and analyse the problems of computation and storage trade-off in the cloud. Based on the requirements identified, we propose a novel concept of Data Dependency Graph (DDG) and propose an effective data sets storage cost model in the cloud. DDG is based on data provenance, which records the generation relationship of all the data sets. With DDG, we know how to effectively regenerate data sets in the cloud and can further calculate their generation costs. The total application cost for the generated data sets includes both their generation cost and their storage cost.

Based on the cost model, we develop novel algorithms which can calculate the minimum cost for storing data sets in the cloud, i.e. the best trade-off between computation and storage. This minimum cost is a benchmark for evaluating the cost-effectiveness of different storage strategies in the cloud. For different situations, we develop different benchmarking approaches with polynomial time complexity for a seemingly NP-hard problem, where (1) the static on-demand approach is for situations in which only occasional benchmarking is requested; and (2) the dynamic on-the-fly approach is suitable for situations in which more frequent benchmarking is requested at runtime.

We develop novel cost-effective storage strategies for users to facilitate at runtime of the cloud. These are different from the minimum cost benchmarking approach, and sometimes users may have certain preferences regarding storage of some particular data sets due to reasons other than cost – e.g. guaranteeing immediate access to certain data sets. Hence, users' preferences should also be considered in a storage strategy. Based on these considerations, we develop two cost-effective storage strategies for different situations: (1) the cost-rate-based strategy is highly efficient with fairly reasonable cost-effectiveness; and (2) the local-optimisation-based strategy is highly cost-effective with very reasonable time complexity.

To the best of our knowledge, this book is the first comprehensive and systematic work investigating the issue of computation and storage trade-off in the cloud in order to reduce the overall application cost. By proposing innovative concepts, theorems and algorithms, the major contribution of this book is that it helps bring the cost down dramatically for both cloud users and service providers to run computation and data-intensive scientific applications in the cloud.

1 Introduction

This book investigates the trade-off between computation and storage in the cloud. This is a brand new and significant issue for deploying applications with the pay-as-you-go model in the cloud, especially computation and data-intensive scientific applications. The novel research reported in this book is for both cloud service providers and users to reduce the cost of storing large generated application data sets in the cloud. A suite consisting of a novel cost model, benchmarking approaches and storage strategies is designed and developed with the support of new concepts, solid theorems and innovative algorithms. Experimental evaluation and case study demonstrate that our work helps bring the cost down dramatically for running the computation and data-intensive scientific applications in the cloud.

This chapter introduces the background and key issues of this research. It is organised as follows. Section 1.1 gives a brief introduction to running scientific applications in the cloud. Section 1.2 outlines the key issues of this research. Finally, Section 1.3 presents an overview for the remainder of this book.

1.1 Scientific Applications in the Cloud

Running scientific applications usually requires not only high-performance computing (HPC) resources but also massive storage [34]. In many scientific research fields, like astronomy [33], high-energy physics [61] and bioinformatics [65], scientists need to analyse a large amount of data either from existing data resources or collected from physical devices. During these processes, large amounts of new data might also be generated as intermediate or final products [34]. Scientific applications are usually data intensive [36,61], where the generated data sets are often terabytes or even petabytes in size. As reported by Szalay et al. in [74], science is in an exponential world and the amount of scientific data will double every year over the next decade and on into the future. Producing scientific data sets involves a large number of computation-intensive tasks, e.g., with scientific workflows [35], and hence takes a long time for execution. These generated data sets contain important intermediate or final results of the computation, and need to be stored as valuable resources. This is because (i) data can be reused — scientists may need to re-analyse the results or apply new analyses on the existing data sets [16] — and (ii) data can be shared — for collaboration, the computation results may be shared, hence the data sets are used by scientists from different institutions [19]. Storing valuable generated application data sets can save their regeneration cost when they are reused, not to mention the waiting time caused by regeneration. However, the large size of the scientific data sets presents a serious challenge in terms of storage. Hence, popular scientific applications are often deployed in grid or HPC systems [61] because they have HPC resources and/or massive storage. However, building and maintaining a grid or HPC system is extremely expensive and neither can easily be made available for scientists all over the world to utilise.

In recent years, cloud computing is emerging as the latest distributed computing paradigm which provides redundant, inexpensive and scalable resources on demand to system requirements [42]. Since late 2007 when the concept of cloud computing was proposed [83], it has been utilised in many areas with a certain degree of success [17,21,45,62]. Meanwhile, cloud computing adopts a pay-as-you-go model where users are charged according to the usage of cloud services such as computation, storage and network[1] services in the same manner as for conventional utilities in everyday life (e.g., water, electricity, gas and telephone) [22]. Cloud computing systems offer a new way to deploy computation and data-intensive applications. As Infrastructure as a Service (IaaS) is a very popular way to deliver computing resources in the cloud [1], the heterogeneity of the computing systems [92] of one service provider can be well shielded by virtualisation technology. Hence, users can deploy their applications in unified resources without any infrastructure investment in the cloud, where excessive processing power and storage can be obtained from commercial cloud service providers. Furthermore, cloud computing systems offer a new paradigm in which scientists from all over the world can collaborate and conduct their research jointly. As cloud computing systems are usually based on the Internet, scientists can upload their data and launch their applications in the cloud from anywhere in the world. Furthermore, as all the data are managed in the cloud, it is easy to share data among scientists.

However, new challenges also arise when we deploy a scientific application in the cloud. With the pay-as-you-go model, the resources need to be paid for by users; hence the total application cost for generated data sets in the cloud highly depends on the strategy used to store them. For example, storing all the generated application data sets in the cloud may result in a high storage cost since some data sets may be seldom used but large in size, but if we delete all the generated data sets and regenerate them every time they are needed, the computation cost may also be very high. Hence there should be a trade-off between computation and storage for deploying applications; this is an important and challenging issue in the cloud. By investigating this issue, this research proposes a new cost model, novel benchmarking approaches and innovative storage strategies, which would help both cloud service providers and users to reduce application costs in the cloud.

---

[1] In this book, we investigate only the trade-off between computation and storage, where a network is not incorporated. Please refer to Section 3.2.2 for detailed explanations.

1.2 Key Issues of This Research

In the cloud, the application cost highly depends on the strategy of storing the large generated data sets due to the pay-as-you-go model. A good strategy is to find a balance to selectively store some popular data sets and regenerate the rest when needed, i.e. finding a trade-off between computation and storage. However, the generated application data sets in the cloud often have dependencies; that is, a computation task can operate on one or more data set(s) and generate new one(s). The decision about whether to store or delete an application data set impacts not only the cost of the data set itself but also that of other data sets in the cloud. To achieve the best trade-off and utilise it to reduce the application cost, we need to investigate the following issues:

1. *Cost model*. Users need a new cost model that can represent the amount that they actually spend on their applications in the cloud. Theoretically, users can get unlimited resources from the commercial cloud service providers for both computation and storage. Hence, for the large generated application data sets, users can flexibly choose how many to store and how many to regenerate. Different storage strategies lead to different consumptions of computation and storage resources and ultimately lead to different total application costs. The new cost model should be able to represent the cost of the applications in the cloud, which is the trade-off between computation and storage.

2. *Minimum cost benchmarking approaches*. Based on the new cost model, we need to find the best trade-off between computation and storage, which leads to the theoretical minimum application cost in the cloud. This minimum cost serves as an important benchmark for evaluating the cost-effectiveness of storage strategies in the cloud. For different applications and users, cloud service providers should be able to provide benchmarking services according to their requirements. Hence benchmarking algorithms need to be investigated, so that we develop different benchmarking approaches to meet the requirements of different situations in the cloud.

3. *Cost-effective dataset storage strategies*. By investigating the trade-off between computation and storage, we determine that cost-effective storage strategies are needed for users to use in their applications at run-time in the cloud. Different from benchmarking, in practice, the minimum cost storage strategy may not be the best strategy for the applications in the cloud. First, storage strategies must be efficient enough to be facilitated at run-time in the cloud. Furthermore, users may have certain preferences concerning the storage of some particular data sets (e.g. tolerance of the accessing delay). Hence we need to design cost-effective storage strategies according to different requirements.

1.3 Overview of This Book

In particular, this book includes new concepts, solid theorems and complex algorithms, which form a suite of systematic and comprehensive solutions to deal with the issue of computation and storage trade-off in the cloud and bring cost-effectiveness to the applications for both users and cloud service providers. The remainder of this book is organised as follows.

In Chapter 2, we introduce the work related to this research. We start by introducing data management in some traditional scientific application systems, especially in grid systems, and then we move to the cloud. By introducing some typical cloud systems for scientific application, we raise the issue of cost-effectiveness in the cloud. Next, we introduce some works that also touch upon the issue of computation and storage trade-off and analyse the differences to ours. Finally, we introduce some works on the subject of data provenance which are the important foundation for our own work.

In Chapter 3, we first introduce a motivating example: a real-world scientific application from astrophysics that is used for searching for pulsars in the universe. Based on this example, we identify and analyse our research problems.

In Chapter 4, we first give a classification of the application data in the cloud and propose an important concept of data dependency graph (DDG). DDG is built on data provenance which depicts the generation relationships of the data sets in the cloud. Based on DDG, we propose a new cost model for datasets storage in the cloud.

In Chapter 5, we develop novel minimum cost benchmarking approaches with algorithms for the best trade-off between computation and storage in the cloud. We propose two approaches, namely static on-demand benchmarking and dynamic on-the-fly benchmarking, to accommodate different application requirements in the cloud.

In Chapter 6, we develop innovative cost-effective storage strategies for user to facilitate at run-time in the cloud. According to different user requirements, we design different strategies accordingly, i.e. a highly efficient cost-rate-based strategy and a highly cost-effective local-optimisation-based strategy.

In Chapter 7, we demonstrate experiment results to evaluate our work as described in the entire book. First, we introduce our cloud computing simulation environment, i.e. SwinCloud. Then we conduct general random simulations to evaluate the performance of our benchmarking approaches and storage strategies. Finally, we demonstrate a case study of the pulsar searching application in which all the research outcomes presented in this book are utilised.

Finally, in Chapter 8, we summarise the new ideas presented in this book and the major contributions of this research.

In order to improve the readability of this book, we have included a notation index in Appendix A; all proofs of theories, lemmas and corollaries in Appendix B; and a related method in Appendix C.

2 Literature Review

This chapter reviews the existing literature related to this research. It is organised as follows. In Section 2.1, we summarise the data management work about scientific applications in the traditional distributed computing systems. In Section 2.2, we first review some existing work about deploying scientific applications in the cloud and raise the issue of cost-effectiveness; we then analyse some research that has touched upon the issue of the trade-off between computation and storage and point out the differences to our work. In Section 2.3, we introduce some work about data provenance which is the important foundation for our work.

2.1 Data Management of Scientific Applications in Traditional Distributed Systems

Alongside the development of information technology (IT), e-science has also become increasingly popular. Since scientific applications are often computation and data intensive, they are now usually deployed in distributed systems to obtain high-performance computing resources and massive storage. Roughly speaking, one can make a distinction between two subgroups in the traditional distributed systems [11]: clusters (including the HPC system) and grids.

Early studies about data management of scientific applications are in cluster computing systems [9]. Since cluster computing is a relative homogenous environment that has a tightly coupled structure, data management in clusters is usually straightforward. The application data are commonly stored according to the system's capacity and moved within the cluster via a fast Ethernet connection while the applications execute.

Grid computing systems [40] are more heterogeneous than clusters. Given the similarity of grid and cloud [42], we mainly investigate the existing related work about grid computing systems in this section. First, we present some general data management technologies in grid. Then, we investigate the data management in some grid workflow systems which are often utilised for running scientific applications. Finally, we briefly introduce the data management technologies in some other distributed systems.

2.1.1 Data Management in Grid

Grid computing has many similarities with cloud computing [80,83]. Both of them are heterogeneous computing environments for large-scale applications. Data management technology in grid, data grid [28] in short, could be a valuable reference for cloud data management. Next, some important features of a data grid are briefly summarised, and some successful systems are also briefly introduced.

Data grid [78] primarily deals with providing services and infrastructure for distributed data-intensive applications that need to access, transfer and modify massive data sets stored in distributed storage resources. Generally speaking, it should have the following capabilities: (a) the ability to search through numerous available data sets for the required data set and to discover suitable data resources for accessing the data, (b) the ability to transfer large-size data sets between resources as fast as possible, (c) the ability for users to manage multiple copies of their data, (d) the ability to select suitable computational resources and process data on them and (e) the ability to manage access permissions for the data.

Grid technology was very popular in the late 1990s and early 2000s because it is suitable for large-scale computation and data-intensive applications. Many data management systems were developed and gained great success. Some of the most successful ones are listed below, and some of them have already been utilised in scientific applications.

Grid Datafarm [75] is a tightly coupled architecture for storage in the grid environment. The architecture consists of nodes that have large disc space. Between the nodes there are interconnections via fast Ethernet. It also has a corresponding file system, process scheduler and parallel I/O APIs (Input/Output Application Programming Interface).

GDMP (Grid Data Mirroring Package) [72] mainly focuses on replication in the grid environment, which has been utilised in high-energy physics. It uses the GridFTP technology to achieve high-speed data transfer and provides point-to-point replication capability.

GridDB [58] builds an overlay based on relational database and provides services for large scientific data analysis. It mainly focuses on the software architecture and query processing.

SRB (Storage Resource Broker) [15] organises data into different virtual collections independent of their physical locations. It could provide a unified view of data files in the distributed environment. It is used in the Kepler workflow system.

RLS (P-RLS) (Peer-to-Peer Replication Location Service) [23,26] maintains all the copies of data's physical locations in the system and provides data discovery services. Newly generated data could be dynamically registered in RLS, so that it could be discovered by the tasks. It has been used in Pegasus and Triana workflow systems.

GSB (Grid Service Broker) [79] is designed to mediate access to distributed resources. It could map tasks to resources and monitor task execution. GSB is the foundation of data management in the Gridbus workflow system.

DaltOn [51] is an infrastructure for scientific data management. It supports the syntactic and semantic integration of data from multiple sources.

A comparison of these data management systems is listed in Table 2.1.

Table 2.1 A Comparison of Data Grid

	Grid Datafarm	GDMP	GridDB	SRB	RLS/P-RLS	GSB	DaltOn
Structure model	Centralised hierarchy, tightly coupled	Centralised hierarchy, loosely coupled	Centralised hierarchy, tightly coupled	Decentralised, flat, intermediate	Centralised hierarchy, loosely coupled	Centralised hierarchy, intermediate	Centralised hierarchy, intermediate
Data type	File, fragment	File, data set	Tables, object	Containers, data sets	File, data set	File, data set	File, data set, table, object
Data partition	Arbitrary fragment of any length	Stored as file and data set	Stored in different databases	Stored as file and data set	Stored as files	Stored global wide	Higher level data integration
Distribution model	Replicas managed through metadata catalogue	point-to-point replication capabilities	Distribute data in distributed database mode	Combined physical storage as logical storage resources	Flexible replicas catalogue index for distribution	Use of Globus replica catalogue	Integration of resources in Internet
Overhead of data management	I/O bandwidth	Bandwidth	Query, bandwidth	Not considered	Not considered	Bandwidth, storage	Not considered
Data dependency	Not considered	Not considered	Structured data format	Not considered	Not considered	Not considered	Not considered

Although data grid has some similarities to data management of the cloud, the two are essentially different. At the infrastructure level, grid systems are usually composed of several computing nodes built up with supercomputers, and the computing nodes are usually connected by fast Ethernet or dedicated networks, so that in data grid, efficient data management can be easily achieved with the high-performance hardware. Cloud systems, however, are based on the Internet and normally composed of data centres built up with commodity hardware, where data management is more challenging. More importantly, at the application level, most clouds are commercial systems while the grids are not. The wide utilisation of the pay-as-you-go model in the cloud makes the issue of cost-effectiveness more important than before.

2.1.2 Data Management in Grid Workflows

Scientific applications are typically very complex. They usually have a large number of tasks and need a long time for execution. Workflow technologies are important tools which can be facilitated to automate the executions of applications [34]. Many workflow management systems were developed in grid environments. Some of the most successful ones are listed below as well as the features of their data management:

Kepler [61] is a scientific workflow management system in the grid environment. It points out that control-flow orientation and dataflow orientation are the difference between business and scientific workflows. Kepler has its own actor-oriented data modelling method for large data in the grid environment. It has two grid actors, called FileFetcher and FileStager, respectively. These actors make use of GridFTP [8] to retrieve files from, or move files to, remote locations on the grid. In the run-time data management, Kepler adopts the SRB system [15].

Pegasus [33] is a workflow management system which mainly focuses on data-intensive scientific applications. It has developed some data management algorithms in the grid environment and uses the RLS [26] system as data management at run-time. In Pegasus, data are asynchronously moved to the tasks on demand to reduce the waiting time of the execution and dynamically delete the data that the task no longer needs to reduce the use of storage.

Gridbus [20] is grid toolkit. In this toolkit, the workflow system has several scheduling algorithms for the data-intensive applications in the grid environment based on a grid resource broker [79]. The algorithms are designed based on different theories (genetic algorithm, Markov decision process, set covering problem, Heuristics), to adapt to different use cases.

Taverna [65] is a scientific workflow system for bioinformatics. It proposes a new process definition language, Sculf, which could model application data in a dataflow. It considers workflow as a graph of processors, each of which transfers a set of data inputs into a set of data outputs.

MOTEUR [44] workflow system advances Taverna's data model. It proposes a data composition strategy by defining some specific operations.

ASKALON [84] is a workflow system designed for scheduling. It puts the computing overhead and data transfer overhead together to get a value 'weight'. It does not discriminate the computing resource and data host. ASKALON also has its own process definition language called AGWL.

Triana [31] is a workflow system which is based on a problem-solving environment that enables the data-intensive scientific application to execute. For the grid, it has an independent abstraction middleware layer called the grid application prototype (GAP). This enables users to advertise, discover and communicate with Web and peer-to-peer (P2P) services. Triana also uses the RLS to manage data at run-time.

GridFlow [54] is a workflow system which uses an agent-based system for grid resource management. It considers data transfer to computing resources and archiving to storage resources as kinds of workflow tasks. But in GridFlow, researchers do not discuss these data-related workflow tasks.

In summary, for data management, all the workflow systems mentioned above have concerned the modelling of workflow data at build-time. Workflow data modelling is a long-term research topic in academia with matured theories, including workflow data patterns [69] and dataflow programming language [53]. For data management at workflow run-time, most of these workflow systems simply adopt data management technology in the data grid. They do not consider the dependencies among the application data. Only Pegasus proposes some strategies for workflow data placement based on dependency [27,71], but it has not designed specific algorithms to achieve them. As all these workflow systems are in a grid computing environment, they neither utilise the pay-as-you-go model nor investigate the issue of cost-effectiveness in deploying the applications.

2.1.3 Data Management in Other Distributed Systems

Many technologies are utilised for computation and data-intensive scientific applications in distributed environments and have their own specialties. They could be important references for our work. A brief overview is shown below [78]:

Distributed database (DDB) [68]. A DDB is a logically organised collection of data stored at different sites on a computer network. Each site has a degree of autonomy, which is capable of executing a local application, and also participates in the execution of a global application. A DDB can be formed either by taking an existing single site database and splitting it over different sites (top-down approach) or by federating existing database management systems so that they can be accessed through a uniform interface (bottom-up approach). However, DDBs are mainly designed for storing the structured data, which is not suitable for managing large generated data sets (e.g. raw data saved in files) in scientific applications.

Content delivery network (CDN) [38]. A CDN consists of a 'collection of (non-origin) servers that attempt to offload work from origin servers by delivering content on their behalf'. That is, within a CDN, client requests are satisfied by other servers distributed around the Internet (also called edge servers) that cache the content originally stored at the source (origin) server. The primary aims of a CDN are, therefore, load balancing to reduce effects of sudden surges in requests, bandwidth conservation for objects such as media clips and reducing the round-trip time to serve the content to the client. However, CDNs have not gained wide acceptance for data distribution because of the restricted model that they follow.

P2P Network [66]. The primary aims of a P2P network are to ensure scalability and reliability by removing the centralised authority and also to ensure redundancy, to share resources and to ensure anonymity. Such networks have mainly focused on creating efficient strategies to locate particular files within a group of peers, to provide reliable transfers of such files in the face of high volatility and to manage high load caused by the demand for highly popular files. Currently, major P2P content-sharing networks do not provide an integrated computation and data distribution environment.

2.2 Cost-Effectiveness of Scientific Applications in the Cloud

Nowadays, scientific applications are often deployed in grid systems [61] because they have high performance and massive storage. However, building a grid system is extremely expensive, and it is normally not open to other scientists around the world. When cloud computing was on the horizon [37,80,83], it was deemed the next generation of IT platforms that would be able to deliver computing as a kind of utility [22]. Taking advantage of the new features, cloud computing technology has been utilised in many areas as soon as it is proposed, such as data mining [45], database application [17], parallel computing [46], content delivery [18] and so on.

2.2.1 Cost-Effectiveness of Deploying Scientific Applications in the Cloud

Scientific applications have already been introduced to the cloud, and research on deploying applications in the cloud has become popular [29,55,57,81,88]. A cloud computing system for scientific applications, i.e. science cloud, has already commenced; some successful and representative ones are as follows:

1. The OpenNebula [5] project facilitates on-premise IaaS cloud computing, offering a complete and comprehensive solution for the management of virtualised data centres to enable private, public and hybrid clouds.
2. Nimbus platform [4] is an integrated set of tools that delivers the power and versatility of infrastructure clouds to users. Nimbus platform allows users to combine Nimbus, OpenStack, Amazon and other clouds.
3. Eucalyptus [2] enables the creation of on-premise private clouds, with no requirements for retooling the organisation's existing IT infrastructure or need to introduce specialised hardware.

Foster et al. made a comprehensive comparison of grid computing and cloud computing [42], and two important differences related to this book are as follows:

1. Compared to a grid, cloud computing systems can provide the same high-performance computing resources and massive storage required for scientific applications, but with a

lower infrastructure construction cost, among many other features. This is because cloud computing systems are composed of data centres which can be clusters of commodity hardware [83]. Hence, deploying scientific applications in the cloud could be more cost effective than its grid counterpart.

2. By utilising virtualisation technology, cloud computing systems are more scalable and elastic. Because new hardware can be easily added to the data centres, service providers can deliver cloud services based on the pay-as-you-go model, and users can dynamically scale up or down the computation and storage resources they use.

Based on the new features of cloud, compared to the traditional distributed computing systems like cluster and grid, a cloud computing system has a cost benefit from various aspects [12]. Assunção et al. [13] demonstrate that cloud computing can extend the capacity of clusters with a cost benefit. With Amazon clouds' cost model and BOINC volunteer computing middleware, the work in [56] analyses the cost benefit of cloud computing versus grid computing. The work by Deelman et al. [36] also applies Amazon clouds' cost model and demonstrates that cloud computing offers a cost-effective way to deploy scientific applications. In [49], Hoffa et al. conduct simulations of running an astronomy scientific workflow in cloud and clusters, which shows cloud scientific workflows are cost effective. Meanwhile, Tsakalozos et al. [77] point out that by flexible utilisation of cloud resources, the service provider's profit can also be maximised. Most notably, Cho et al. [30] further propose planning algorithms of how to transfer large amounts of scientific data to commercial clouds in order to run the applications.

The above works mainly focus on the comparison of cloud computing systems and the traditional distributed computing paradigms, which show that applications running in the cloud have cost benefits, but they do not touch the issue of computation and storage trade-off in the cloud.

2.2.2 *Trade-Off Between Computation and Storage in the Cloud*

Based on the work introduced in Section 2.2.1, the research addressed in this book makes a significant step forward regarding the application cost in the cloud. We develop our approaches and strategies by investigating the issue of computation and storage trade-off in the cloud.

This research is mainly inspired by the work in two research areas: cache management and scheduling. With a smart caching mechanism [39,50,52], system performance can be greatly improved. The similarity is that both pre-store some data for future use, while the difference is that caching is used to reduce data-accessing delays; however, our work is to reduce the application cost in the cloud. Works in scheduling focus on reducing various costs for either applications [82] or systems [86], but they investigate this issue from the perspective of resource provisioning and utilisation, not from the trade-off between computation and storage. In [43], Garg et al. investigate the trade-off between time and cost in the cloud, where users can reduce the computation time by using expensive CPU (central processing unit) instances with higher performance. This trade-off is different from ours, which aims to reduce the application cost in the cloud.

As the trade-off between computation and storage is an important issue, some researches have already embarked on this issue to a certain extent. The Nectar system [48] is designed for automatic management of data and computation in data centres, where obsolete data sets are deleted and regenerated whenever reused in order to improve resource utilisation. In [36], Deelman et al. present that storing some frequently used intermediate data can reduce the cost in comparison to always regenerating them from the input data. In [7], Adams et al. propose a model to represent the trade-off of computation cost and storage cost, but they have not given any strategy to find this trade-off.

In this book, for the first time, the issue of computation and storage trade-off for scientific data set storage in the cloud is comprehensively and systematically investigated. We propose a new cost model to represent this trade-off, develop novel minimum cost benchmarking approaches to find the best trade-off [90] and design novel cost-effective data set storage strategies based on this trade-off for users to store the application data sets [87,89,91].

2.3   Data Provenance in Scientific Applications

The research works on data provenance form an important foundation for our work. Data provenance is a kind of important metadata in which the dependencies among application data sets are recorded [70]. The dependency depicts the generation relationship among the data sets. For scientific applications, data provenance is especially important because after the execution, some application data sets may be deleted, but sometimes the users have to regenerate them for either reuse or reanalysis [16]. Data provenance records the information on how the data sets were generated, which is very important for our research on the trade-off between computation and storage.

Due to the importance of data provenance in scientific applications, much research on recording data provenance of the system has been conducted [14,47]. For example, some of them are for scientific workflow systems [14]. Some popular scientific workflow systems, such as Kepler [61], have their own system to record provenance during workflow execution [10]. Recently, research on data provenance in cloud computing systems has also appeared [63]. More specifically, Osterweil et al. [67] present how to generate a data derivation graph for the execution of a scientific workflow, where one graph records the data provenance of one execution, and Foster et al. [41] propose the concept of *virtual data* in the Chimera system, which enables automatic regeneration of data sets when needed.

2.4   Summary

In this chapter, the literatures of recent studies related to data management of scientific applications are reviewed. We start with the grid systems and then move on to the cloud. By investigating typical grid and cloud systems, we analyse the cost-effectiveness of deploying scientific applications in the cloud. Meanwhile, based on the literature review, we demonstrate that the core research issues of this book, i.e. computation and storage trade-off, are significant yet barely touched in the cloud. Finally, we introduce some works about data provenance which are an important foundation for our work.

3 Motivating Example and Research Issues

The research in this book is motivated by a real-world scientific application. In this chapter, Section 3.1 introduces a motivating example of a pulsar searching application from astrophysics; Section 3.2 analyses the problems and challenges of deploying scientific applications in the cloud; Section 3.3 describes the specific research issues of this book in detail.

3.1 Motivating Example

The Swinburne Astrophysics group has been conducting pulsar searching surveys using the observation data from the Parkes Radio Telescope, which is one of the most famous radio telescopes in the world.[1] Pulsar searching is a typical scientific application. It involves complex and time-consuming tasks and needs to process terabytes of data. Figure 3.1 depicts a high-level structure of the pulsar searching workflow, which is currently running at the Swinburne high-performance super-computing facility.[2] There are three major steps in the pulsar searching process:

1. *Raw signal data recording.* In the Parkes Radio Telescope, there are 13 embedded beam receivers by which signals from the universe are received. At the beginning, raw signal data are *recorded* at a rate of 1 GB per second by the ATNF[3] Parkes Swinburne Recorder.[4] Depending on different areas in the universe in which the scientists want to conduct the pulsar searching survey, the observation time is normally from 4 min to 1 h. The raw signal data are pre-processed by a local cluster at Parkes in real time and archived in tapes for permanent storage and future analysis.

2. *Data preparation for pulsar seeking.* The raw signal data recorded from the telescope are interleaved from multiple beams, so at the beginning of the workflow, different beam files are *extracted* from the raw data files and *compressed*. They are normally 1 GB to 20 GB each in size depending on the observation time. The scientists analyse the beam files to find the contained pulsar signals. However, the signals are dispersed by the interstellar medium, and to counteract this effect the scientists have to conduct a *de-disperse* step. Since the potential dispersion source is unknown, a large number of de-dispersion

---

[1] http://www.parkes.atnf.csiro.au/.
[2] http://astronomy.swin.edu.au/supercomputing/.
[3] http://www.atnf.csiro.au/.
[4] http://astronomy.swin.edu.au/pulsar/?topic=apsr.

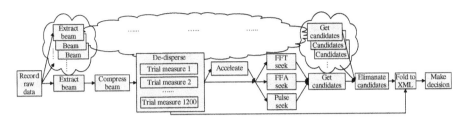

Figure 3.1 Pulsar searching workflow.

files need to be generated with different dispersion trials. For one dispersion trial of one beam file, the size of the de-dispersion file is approximately 4.6 MB to 80 MB depending on the size of the input beam file (1 GB to 20 GB). In the current pulsar searching survey, 1200 is the minimum number of the dispersion trials, where this de-dispersion step takes 1 h to 13 h to finish and generates around 5 GB to 90 GB of de-dispersion files. Furthermore, for binary pulsar searching, every de-dispersion file needs a separate *accelerate* step for processing. This step generates the accelerated de-dispersion files of similar size in the *de-disperse* step.

3. *Pulsar seeking.* Based on the generated de-dispersion files, different seeking algorithms can be applied to search for pulsar candidates, such as *fast fourier transform (FFT) seeking, fast fold algorithm (FFA) seeking* and *single pulse seeking.* For example, the *FFT seeking* algorithm takes 7 min to 80 min to seek the 1200 de-dispersion files with different sizes (5 GB to 90 GB). A candidate list of pulsars is generated after the seeking step, which is saved in a text file, normally 1 KB in size. Furthermore, by comparing the candidates generated from different beam files in a simultaneous time session, interference may be detected and some candidates may be *eliminated.* With the final pulsar candidates, we need to go back to the de-dispersion files to find their feature signals and *fold* them to XML files. Each candidate is saved in a separated XML file about 25 KB in size. This step takes up to 1 h depending on the number of candidates found in this searching process. Finally, the XML files are visually displayed to scientists for *making decisions* on whether a pulsar has been found or not.

At present, all the generated data sets are deleted after having been used, and the scientists only store the raw beam data, which are extracted from the raw telescope data. Whenever there is a need to use the deleted data sets, the scientists will regenerate them based on the raw beam files. The generated data sets are not stored, mainly because the supercomputer is a shared facility that cannot offer sufficient storage capacity to hold the accumulated terabytes of data. However, it is better to store some data sets. For example, the de-dispersion files can be more frequently used, and based on them, the scientists can apply different seeking algorithms to find potential pulsar candidates. For the large input beam files, the regeneration of the de-dispersion files will take more than 10 h. This not only delays the scientists from conducting their experiments but also requires a lot of computation resources. However, some data sets may not need to be stored. For example, the accelerated de-dispersion files, which are generated by the *accelerate* step, are not often used. The *accelerate* step is an optional step that is only used for binary pulsar searching. In light of this, and given the large size of these data sets, they may be not worth storing as it could be more cost effective to regenerate them from the de-dispersion files whenever they are required.

3.2 Problem Analysis

Traditionally, scientific applications are normally deployed on the high-performance computing facilities, such as clusters and grids. Scientific applications are often complex with huge data sets generated during their execution. The question of how to store these data sets is often decided by the scientists themselves who use the scientific applications. This is because the clusters and grids only serve for certain institutions. The scientists may store the data sets that are most valuable to them based on the storage capacity of the system. However, for many scientific applications, the storage capacities are limited, such as the pulsar searching workflow introduced in Section 3.1. The scientists have to delete all the generated data sets because of the storage limitation. To store large scientific data sets, scientific communities have to set up data repositories [73] with a large infrastructure investment. However, the storage bottleneck can be avoided in a cost-effective way if we deploy scientific applications in the cloud.

3.2.1 Requirements and Challenges of Deploying Scientific Applications in the Cloud

In a commercial cloud computing environment [1], theoretically, the system can offer unlimited storage resources. All the data sets generated by the scientific applications can be stored if the users (e.g. scientists) are willing to pay for the required resources. However, new requirements and challenges also emerge for deploying scientific applications in the cloud, which are summarised as follows. Hence, whether to store the generated data sets or not is no longer an easy decision.

1. All the resources in the cloud carry certain costs, so whether we are storing or generating a data set, we have to pay for the resources used. The application data sets vary in size and have different generation costs and usage frequencies. Some of them may be used often whilst some others may not. On one extreme, it is most likely not cost effective to store all the generated data sets in the cloud. On the other extreme, if we delete them all, regeneration of frequently used data sets most likely imposes a high computation cost. We need a mechanism to balance the regeneration cost and the storage cost of the application data, in order to reduce the total application cost for data set storage. This is also the core issue of this book, i.e. the trade-off between computation and storage.

2. The best trade-off between computation and storage cost may not be the best strategy for storing application data. When the deleted data sets are needed, the regeneration not only imposes computation costs but also causes a time delay. Depending on the different time constraints of applications [24,25], users' tolerance of this computation may differ

dramatically. Sometimes users may want the data to be available immediately and would pay a higher cost for storing some particular data sets; sometimes users do not care about waiting for data to become available, hence they may delete the seldom-used data set to reduce the overall application cost. Hence, we need to incorporate users' preferences on data storage into this research.

3. Scientists cannot predict the usage frequencies of the application data anymore. For a single research group, if the data resources of the applications are only used by their own scientists, the scientists may estimate the usage frequencies of the data sets and decide whether to store or delete them. However, the cloud is normally not developed for a single scientist or institution but rather for scientists from different institutions to collaborate and share data resources. Scientists from all over the world can easily visit the cloud via Internet to launch their applications, and all the application data are managed in the cloud. This requires data management to be automatic. Hence, we need to investigate the trade-off between computation and storage for all the users, which can reduce the overall application cost. More specifically, the data sets usage frequencies should be discovered and obtained from the system logs, rather than manually set by the users. However, forecasting accurate data sets' usage frequencies is beyond the scope of this research, and we list it as our future work in Section 8.3. In this book, we assume that the data sets' usage frequencies have already been obtained from the system logs.

3.2.2 Bandwidth Cost of Deploying Scientific Applications in the Cloud

Bandwidth is another common type of resource in the cloud. As cloud computing is such a fast-growing market, more and more different cloud service providers will appear. In the future, we will be able to more flexibly select service providers to conduct our applications based on their pricing models. An intuitive idea is to incorporate different cloud service providers for applications: we can store the data with one provider who offers a lower price for storage resources and choose another provider who offers a lower price for computation resources to run the computation tasks. However, at present, normally it is not practical to run scientific applications across different cloud service providers for the following reasons:

1. The data in scientific applications are often very large in size. They are too large to be transferred efficiently via the Internet. Due to bandwidth limitations of the Internet, in today's scientific projects, delivery of hard discs is a common practice to transfer application data, and it is also considered to be the most efficient way to transfer, say, terabytes of data [12]. Currently, express delivery companies can deliver the hard discs nationwide by the end of the next day and worldwide in 2 or 3 days. In contrast, transferring 1 TB data via the Internet would take more than 10 days at a speed of 1 MB/s. To break the bandwidth limitation, some institutions set up dedicated optic fibres to transfer data. For example, Swinburne University of Technology has built a dedicated fibre to the Parkes telescope station with gigabits of bandwidth. However, it is mainly used for transferring gigabytes of data. To transfer terabytes, or petabytes, of data, scientists would still prefer to ship hard discs. Furthermore, building (dedicated) fibre connections is very expensive, and they are not yet widely used in the Internet. Hence, transferring scientific application data between different cloud service providers via the Internet is not efficient.

2. Cloud service providers place a high price on data transfer in and out their data centres. In contrast, data transfers within one cloud service provider's data centres are usually

free. For example, the data transfer price of Amazon's cloud service is US$0.12 per GB[5] of data transferred out. Compared with the storage price of US$0.15 per GB per month,[6] the data transfer price is relatively high, so finding a cheaper storage cloud service provider and transferring data may not be cost effective. In cloud service providers' defence, they charge a high price on data transfer not only because of the bandwidth limitation but also as a business strategy. As data are deemed an important resource today, cloud service providers want users to keep all the application data in their storage cloud. For example, Amazon places a zero price on data transferred into its data centres, which means users could upload their data to Amazon's cloud storage for free. However, the price of data transferred out of Amazon is not only not free but also rather expensive.

Due to the reasons above, we assume that the scientists only utilise cloud services from one service provider to deploy their applications. Furthermore, according to some research [36,49], the cost-effective way of doing science in the cloud is to upload all the application data to the cloud storage and run all the applications with the cloud services. So we assume that the scientists upload all the original data to the cloud to conduct their processing. Hence, the cost of transferring data in and out of the cloud depends only on the applications themselves (i.e. how much original and result data the applications have) and has no impact on the usage of computation and storage resources for running the applications in the cloud. Hence, we do not incorporate data transfer cost in the trade-off between computation and storage at this stage.

3.3 Research Issues

In this section, we discuss the research issues tackled in this book based on the problems analysed in Section 3.2.

3.3.1 Cost Model for Data Set Storage in the Cloud

In a commercial cloud, in theory, users can get unlimited resources for both computation and storage. However, they are responsible for the cost of the resources used due to the pay-as-you-go model. Hence, users need a new and appropriate cost model that can represent the cost that they actually incur on their applications in the cloud.

For the large generated application data sets in the cloud, users can be given the choice to store them for future use or delete them to save the storage cost. Different storage strategies lead to different consumptions of storage and computation resources and finally lead to different total application costs. Furthermore, because there are dependencies among the application data sets (i.e. a computation

---

[5] http://aws.amazon.com/ec2/pricing/ — The prices may fluctuate from time to time according to market factors.

[6] http://aws.amazon.com/s3/pricing/ — The prices may fluctuate from time to time according to market factors.

task can operate on one or more data sets and generate one or more new ones), the storage status of a data set is dependent not only on its own generation and storage costs but also on the storage status of its predecessors and successors. The new cost model should be able to represent the total cost of the applications based on the trade-off between computation and storage in the cloud, where data dependencies are taken into account.

3.3.2 Minimum Cost Benchmarking Approaches

Minimum cost benchmarking is to find the *theoretical* minimum application cost based on the cost model, which is also the best trade-off between computation and storage in the cloud. Due to the pay-as-you-go model in the cloud, cost is one of the most important factors that users care about. As a rapidly increasing number of data sets is generated and stored in the cloud, users need to evaluate the cost-effectiveness of their storage strategies. Hence, the service providers should be able to (and need to!) provide benchmarking services that can inform the minimum cost of storing the application data sets in the cloud.

Calculating the minimum cost benchmark is a seemingly NP-hard problem because there are complex dependencies among the data sets in the cloud. Furthermore, this application cost in the cloud is of a dynamic value. This is because of the dynamic nature of the cloud computing system, i.e. (a) new data sets may be generated in the cloud at any time, and (b) the usage frequencies of the data sets may also change as time goes on. Hence, the minimum cost benchmark may change from time to time. In order to guarantee the quality of service (QoS) in the cloud, there should be different benchmarking approaches accommodating different situations. For example, in some applications, users may only need to know the benchmark before or occasionally during application execution. In this situation, benchmarking should be provided as a static service which can respond to users' requests on demand. However, in some applications, users may have more frequent benchmarking requests at run time. In this situation, benchmarking should be provided as a dynamic service which can respond to users' requests on the fly.

3.3.3 Cost-Effective Storage Strategies

Based on the trade-off between computation and storage, cost-effective storage strategies need to be designed in this book. Different from benchmarking, *in practice*, the minimum cost storage strategy may not be the best strategy for the applications because storage strategies are for users to use at run time in the cloud and should take users' preferences into consideration.

Besides cost-effectiveness, storage strategies must be efficient enough to be facilitated at run time in the cloud. For different applications, the requirements of efficiency may be different. On the one hand, some applications may need highly efficient storage strategies with acceptable though not optimal cost-effectiveness. On the other hand, some applications may need highly cost-effective storage strategies with acceptable efficiency. According to different requirements, we need to design corresponding storage strategies.

Furthermore, to reflect users' preferences on the data sets' storage, we need to incorporate related parameters into the strategies which (a) guarantee all the application data sets' regenerations can fulfil users' tolerance of data-accessing delay, and (b) allow users to store some data sets according to their preferences.

3.4 Summary

In this chapter, based on a real-world pulsar searching scientific application from astrophysics, we analyse the requirements of data storage in scientific applications and how cloud computing systems can fulfil these requirements. Then we analyse the problems of deploying scientific applications in the cloud and define the scope of this research. Based on the analysis, we present the detailed research issues of this book: (a) a cost model for data set storage in the cloud, (b) minimum cost benchmarking approaches and (c) practical data set storage strategies.

4 Cost Model of Data Set Storage in the Cloud

In this section, we present our new cost model of data set storage in the cloud. Specifically, Section 4.1 introduces a classification of application data in the cloud and further expresses the scope of this research. Section 4.2 introduces data provenance and describes the concept of data dependency graph, which is used to depict the data dependencies in the cloud. Based on Sections 4.1 and 4.2, in Section 4.3 we describe the new cost model and its important attributes in detail.

The cost model that has been utilised in our work is presented in [87,89,90,91].

4.1 Classification of Application Data in the Cloud

In general, there are two types of data stored in the cloud storage — *original data* and *generated data*:

1. *Original data* are the data uploaded by users, and in scientific applications they are usually the raw data collected from the devices in the experiments. In the cloud, they are the initial input of the applications for processing and analysis. The most important feature of these data is that if they are deleted, they cannot be regenerated by the system.
2. *Generated data* are the data produced in the cloud computing system while the applications run. They are the intermediate or final computation results of the application which can be used in the future. The most important feature of these data is that they can be regenerated by the system — and more efficiently so if we know their provenance.

For *original data*, only the users can decide whether they should be stored or deleted because they cannot be regenerated once deleted. Hence, our research only focuses on *generated data* in the cloud where the system can automatically decide their storage status for achieving the best trade-off between computation and storage. In this book, we refer to *generated data* as data set(s).

4.2 Data Provenance and DDG

Scientific applications have many computation and data-intensive tasks that generate many data sets of considerable size. There exist dependencies among these data sets, which depict the generation (also known as derivation) relationships. For scientific applications, some data sets may be deleted after the execution, but if so, sometimes they need to be regenerated for either reuse or reanalysis [16]. To regenerate a data set in the cloud, we need to find its stored predecessors and start the computation from them. Hence, the regeneration of a data set includes not only the computation of the data set itself but also the regeneration of its deleted predecessors, if any. This makes minimising the total application cost a very complex problem.

Data provenance is a kind of important metadata which records the dependencies among data sets [70], i.e. the information of how the data sets were generated. Data provenance is especially important for scientific applications in the cloud because the regeneration of data sets from the original data may be very time consuming and therefore carry a high cost. With data provenance information, the regeneration of the requested data set could start from some stored (predecessor) data sets and hence be more efficient and cost effective.

Taking the advantage of data provenance, we can build a DDG. The references for all the data sets generated (or modified) in the cloud, whether stored or deleted, are recorded in the DDG as different nodes. In DDG, every node denotes a data set. Figure 4.1 shows a simple DDG, where every node in the graph denotes a data set. Data set d_1 pointing to data set d_2 means that d_1 is used to generate d_2, and d_2 pointing to d_3 and d_5 means that d_2 is used to generate d_3 and d_5 based on different operations; data sets d_4 and d_6 pointing to data set d_7 means that d_4 and d_6 are used together to generate d_7.

DDG is a directed acyclic graph (DAG). This is because DDG records the provenances of how data sets are derived in the system as time goes on. In other words, it depicts the generation relationships of data sets. When some of the deleted data sets need to be reused, in general, we need not regenerate them from the original data. With DDG, the system can find the predecessors of the requested data set, so that they can be regenerated from their nearest stored predecessors.

We denote a data set d_i in DDG as $d_i \in DDG$, and to better describe the relationships of data sets in DDG, we define two symbols $\rightarrow$ and $\leftrightarrow$:

- $\rightarrow$ denotes that two data sets have a generation relationship, where $d_i \rightarrow d_j$ means that d_i is a predecessor data set of d_j in the DDG. For example, in the DDG depicted in Figure 4.1, we have $d_1 \rightarrow d_2$, $d_1 \rightarrow d_4$, $d_5 \rightarrow d_7$, $d_1 \rightarrow d_7$ and so on. Furthermore, $\rightarrow$ is transitive, i.e.

$$d_i \rightarrow d_j \rightarrow d_k \Leftrightarrow d_i \rightarrow d_j \wedge d_j \rightarrow d_k \Rightarrow d_i \rightarrow d_k$$

- $\leftrightarrow$ denotes that two data sets do not have a generation relationship, where $d_i \leftrightarrow d_j$ means that d_i and d_j are in different branches in DDG. For example, in the DDG depicted in Figure 4.1, we have $d_3 \leftrightarrow d_5$, $d_3 \leftrightarrow d_6$ and so on. Furthermore, $\leftrightarrow$ is commutative, i.e. $d_i \leftrightarrow d_j \Leftrightarrow d_j \leftrightarrow d_i$.

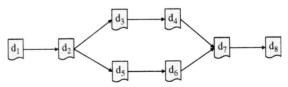

Figure 4.1 A simple DDG.

4.3   Data Set Storage Cost Model in the Cloud

In a commercial cloud computing environment, if the users want to deploy and run applications, they need to pay for the resources used. The resources are offered by cloud service providers, who have their cost models to charge the users on storage and computation. For example, one set of Amazon cloud services' prices is as follows[1]:

- US$0.15 per gigabyte per month for the storage resources,
- US$0.1 per CPU instance hour for the computation resources.

In this book, in order to represent the trade-off between computation and storage, we define the total cost for running a scientific application in the cloud as follows:

$$Cost = computation + storage$$

where the total cost of the application, cost, is the sum of computation, which is the total cost of computation resources used to regenerate data sets, and storage, which is the total cost of storage resources used to store the data sets. As indicated in Section 4.1, our research only focuses on the generated data. The total application cost in this book does not include computation cost of the application itself and the storage cost of the original data.

To calculate the total application cost in the cloud, we define some important attributes for the data sets in DDG. For data set d_i, its attributes are denoted as $\langle x_i, y_i, f_i, v_i, provSet_i, CostR_i \rangle$, where

- x_i denotes the generation cost of data set d_i from its direct predecessors. To calculate this generation cost, we have to multiply the time of generating data set d_i by the price of computation resources. Normally, the generation time can be obtained from the system logs.
- y_i denotes the cost of storing data set d_i in the system per time unit (i.e. storage cost rate). This storage cost rate can be calculated by multiplying the size of data set d_i and the price of storage resources per time unit.
- f_i is a flag, which denotes the status whether this data set is stored in or deleted from the system.
- v_i denotes the usage frequency, which indicates how often d_i is used. In cloud computing systems, data sets may be shared by many users from the Internet. Hence, v_i cannot be defined by a single user and should be an estimated value from d_i's usage history recorded in the system logs.
- $provSet_i$ denotes the set of stored provenances that are needed when regenerating data set d_i. In other words, it is the set of references of stored predecessor data sets that are adjacent to d_i in the DDG. If we want to regenerate d_i, we have to find its direct predecessors, which may also be deleted, so we have to further find the stored predecessors of d_i. $provSet_i$ is the set of the nearest stored predecessors of d_i in the DDG.

[1] The prices may fluctuate from time to time according to market factors.

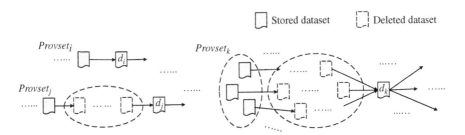

Figure 4.2 A data set's *provSet*s in a DDG in different situations.

Figure 4.2 shows the *provSet*s of a data set in different situations. Formally, we can describe data set d_i's *ProvSet$_i$* as follows:

$$provSet_i = \{d_j \mid \forall\, d_j \in \text{DDG} \wedge f_j = \text{"stored"} \wedge d_j \rightarrow d_i$$
$$\wedge ((\neg \exists d_k \in \text{DDG} \wedge d_j \rightarrow d_k \rightarrow d_i)$$
$$\vee (\exists d_k \in \text{DDG} \wedge d_j \rightarrow d_k \rightarrow d_i \wedge f_k = \text{"deleted"}))\}$$

provSet is a very important attribute of a data set in calculating its generation cost. When we want to regenerate a data set in DDG, we have to start the computation from the data set in its *provSet*. Hence, for data set d_i, its generation cost is:

$$genCost(d_i) = x_i + \sum_{\{d_k \mid d_j \in provSet_i \wedge d_j \rightarrow d_k \rightarrow d_i\}} x_k \tag{4.1}$$

This cost is a total cost of (a) the generation cost of data set d_i from its direct predecessor data sets and (b) the generation costs of d_i's deleted predecessors that need to be regenerated as well.

- *CostR$_i$* is d_i's cost rate, which means the average cost per time unit of the data set d_i in the system. If d_i is a stored data set, then $CostR_i = y_i$. If d_i is a deleted data set in the system, when we need to use d_i, we have to regenerate it. So we multiply the generation cost of d_i by its usage frequency and use this value as the cost rate of d_i in the system, i.e. $CostR_i = genCost(d_i)*v_i$. The storage statuses of the data sets have significant impacts on their cost rates. Formally, data set d_i's cost rate is:

$$CostR_i = \begin{cases} y_i, & f_i = \text{"stored"} \\ genCost(d_i) * v_i, & f_i = \text{"deleted"} \end{cases} \tag{4.2}$$

Based on the definition of the attributes above, we can calculate the total cost rate of storing the data sets recorded in a DDG, which is $\sum_{d_i \in \text{DDG}} CostR_i$. This cost rate is the cost of computation and storage resources consumption in the cloud per time unit, which is also the cost of running the application in the cloud per time unit. Given a time duration t, the total application cost of storing the data sets recorded in a DDG is the integral of the cost rate in this duration as a function of time t, which is

$$Total\_Cost = \int_t \left(\sum_{d_i \in DDG} CostR_i \right) \cdot dt \qquad (4.3)$$

We further define the storage strategy of a DDG as S, where S is a set of data sets in the DDG denoted as $S \subseteq DDG$, which means storing the data sets in S in the cloud and deleting the rest. We denote the sum of cost rates of storing the data sets recorded in a DDG with the storage strategy S as SCR (sum of cost rates), formally:

$$SCR = \left(\sum_{d_i \in DDG} CostR_i \right)_S \qquad (4.4)$$

Based on the definition above, different storage strategies lead to different cost rates (i.e. cost per time unit) for the application in the cloud. This cost rate is the total consumption of computation and storage resources in the cloud per time unit; hence it represents the trade-off between computation and storage. Our work aims at minimising this cost rate so that we can help both service providers and users to reduce the application cost in the cloud.

4.4 Summary

In this chapter, we first introduce a classification of the application data in the cloud, i.e. original data and generated data, and further point out that our research only focuses on the generated data. Then we describe the concept of DDG, which is very important for data set storage in the cloud. Finally, we present the cost model of data set storage based on DDG, where the total application cost is the sum of the computation cost for regenerating data sets and the storage cost for storing data sets. Furthermore, we use a cost rate (i.e. total consumption of computation and storage resources in the cloud per time unit) to represent the trade-off between computation and storage. By minimising this cost rate, our work aims at cutting the application cost in the cloud, which is presented later.

5 Minimum Cost Benchmarking Approaches

In this chapter, we present our minimum cost benchmarking approaches for the applications in the cloud. The benchmark is the theoretical minimum application cost in the cloud, which is also the best trade-off between computation and storage. As introduced in Section 4.3, we use a cost rate to represent this trade-off (i.e. SCR). Benchmarking is the process of finding the minimum value of this cost rate (i.e. the SCR with the minimum cost storage strategy of the DDG). Due to the complex dependencies among the data sets in the cloud, the DDG is a DAG. Hence calculating the minimum cost benchmark is a seemingly NP-hard problem based on the cost model introduced in Section 4.3. Furthermore, the application cost in the cloud is of a dynamic value. This is because of the dynamic nature of the cloud computing system, i.e. new data sets may be generated in the cloud at any time and the usage frequencies of the data sets may also change as time goes on. Hence the minimum cost benchmark may change from time to time. In this chapter, we present two benchmarking approaches: one static and one dynamic.

Section 5.1 presents a novel static on-demand minimum cost benchmarking approach. This approach is suitable for the situation that no frequent benchmarking is requested. In this situation, the benchmarking should be provided as an on-demand service. Whenever a benchmarking request comes, the corresponding algorithms will be triggered to calculate the minimum cost benchmark, which is a one-time-only computation based on the current status of the application. This section is mainly based on our work presented in [90].

Section 5.2 presents a novel dynamic on-the-fly minimum cost benchmarking approach. This approach is suitable for situations in which more frequent benchmarking is requested at runtime. In this approach, by saving and utilising the pre-calculated results, whenever the application cost changes in the cloud, we can quickly calculate the new minimum cost benchmark. By keeping the benchmark dynamically updated, benchmarking requests can be instantly responded to on the fly.

5.1 Static On-Demand Minimum Cost Benchmarking Approach

In this section, we present our on-demand minimum cost benchmarking approach. Specifically, we describe the novel design of a cost transitive tournament shortest path (CTT-SP)-based algorithm that can find the minimum cost storage strategy (MCSS) for a given DDG. The basic idea of the CTT-SP algorithm is to construct a CTT based on the DDG. In a CTT, we guarantee that the paths from the start data set to the end data set have a one-to-one mapping to the storage strategies of the DDG, and that the length of every path equals the total cost rate of the corresponding storage strategy. Then we can use the well-known Dijkstra shortest path (SP) algorithm (or Dijkstra algorithm for short) to find the SP in the CTT, which in fact represents the MCSS: the cost rate of the MCSS (i.e. SCR) is the minimum cost benchmark.

To describe the approach in detail, in Section 5.1.1 we start with the CTT-SP algorithm for the linear DDG, and then in Section 5.1.2 we expand it to the DDG with one block. Next, in Section 5.1.3, we present the general CTT-SP algorithm for on-demand benchmarking. The experiment results are presented in Chapter 7, jointly with the others.

5.1.1 CTT-SP Algorithm for Linear DDG

Linear DDG means a DDG with no branches, where each data set in the DDG, except the first and last, has only one direct predecessor and successor.

Given a linear DDG, which has data sets $\{d_1, d_2, \ldots, d_n\}$, the CTT-SP algorithm has the following four steps:

Step 1: We add two virtual data sets in the DDG, d_s before d_1 and d_e after d_n, as the start and end data sets, and set $x_s = y_s = 0$ and $x_e = y_e = 0$.

Step 2: We add new directed edges in the DDG to construct the transitive tournament. For every data set in the DDG, we add edges that start from it and point to all its successors. Formally, for data set d_i, it has out-edges to all the data sets in the set of $\{d_j | d_j \in \mathrm{DDG} \wedge d_i \rightarrow d_j\}$, and in-edges from all the data sets in the set of $\{d_k | d_k \in \mathrm{DDG} \wedge d_k \rightarrow d_i\}$. Hence for any two data sets d_i and d_j in the DDG, we have an edge between them, denoted as $e < d_i, d_j >$. Formally,

$$d_i, d_j \in \mathrm{DDG} \wedge d_i \rightarrow d \Rightarrow \exists e < d_i, d_j >$$

Step 3: We set weights to the edges. The reason we call the graph CTT is because the weights of its edges are composed of the cost rates of data sets. For an edge $e < d_i, d_j >$, we denote its weight as $\omega < d_i, d_j >$, which is defined as the sum of cost rates of d_j and the data sets between d_i and d_j, supposing that only d_i and d_j are stored and the rest of the data sets between d_i and d_j are all deleted. Formally:

$$\omega < d_i, d_j > = CostR_j + \sum_{\{d_k | d_k \in \mathrm{DDG} \wedge d_i \rightarrow d_k \rightarrow d_j\}} CostR_k$$

$$= y_j + \sum_{\{d_k | d_k \in \mathrm{DDG} \wedge d_i \rightarrow d_k \rightarrow d_j\}} (genCost(d_k) * v_k) \qquad (5.1)$$

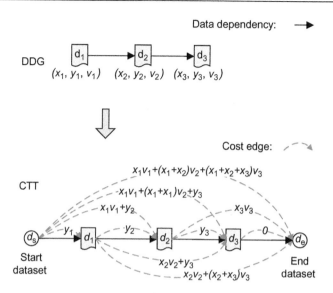

Figure 5.1 An example of constructing CTT.

Since we are discussing the linear DDG, for the data sets between d_i and d_j, d_i is the only data set in their *provSets*. Hence we can further derive:

$$\omega < d_i, d_j > = y_j + \sum_{\{d_k | d_k \in DDG \land d_i \to d_k \to d_j\}} \left(\left(x_k + \sum_{\{d_h | d_h \in DDG \land d_i \to d_h \to d_k\}} x_h \right) * v_k \right)$$

In Figure 5.1, we demonstrate a simple example of constructing CTT for a DDG that has three data sets (d_1, d_2, d_3), where d_s is the start data set that only has out-edges and d_e is the end data set that only has in-edges.

Step 4: We find the SP of CTT. From the construction steps, we can clearly see that the CTT is an acyclic complete oriented graph. Hence we can use the Dijkstra algorithm to find the SP from d_s to d_e. The Dijkstra algorithm is a classic greedy algorithm to find the SP in graph theory. We denote the SP from d_s to d_e as $P_{min} < d_s, d_e >$.

Theorem 5.1 *Given a linear DDG*[1]*with data sets* $\{d_1, d_2, \ldots, d_n\}$, *the length of* $P_{min} < d_s, d_e >$ *of its* CTT *is the minimum cost rate for storing the data sets in the* DDG, *and the corresponding storage strategy is to store the data sets that* $P_{min} < d_s, d_e >$ *traverses.*

Theorem 5.1 demonstrates that the linear CTT-SP algorithm finds the MCSS of linear DDGs; hence it can be used for minimum cost benchmarking. Figure 5.2

---

[1] As indicated at the end of Chapter 1, proofs of all the theorems, lemmas and corollaries are in Appendix B of this book.

Algorithm:	**Linear CTT-SP**	
Input:	Start dataset d_s; End dataset d_e;	
	A linear DDG ;	//include d_s and d_e
Output:	S	//MCSS of the DDG
	SCR	//Minimum cost benchmark

01. **for** (every dataset d_i in DDG)   //Create CTT
02.   **for** (every dataset d_j, where $d_i \rightarrow d_j$)
03.   Create $e < d_i, d_j >$ //Create an edge
04. $weight = 0$;
05.   **for** (every dataset dk, where $d_i \rightarrow d_k \rightarrow d_j$)   //Calculate the weight of an edge
06. $genCost = 0$;
07.   **for** (every dataset dh, where $d_i \rightarrow d_h \rightarrow d_k$)
08. $genCost = genCost + x_h$;
09. $weight = weight + (x_k + genCost)^* v_k$;   //Accumulate generation cost rate
10. $weight = weight + y_j$;
11.   Set $\omega < d_i, d_j >= weight$;   //Set weight to an edge
12. P_{min} = Dijkstra (d_s, d_e, CTT);   //Find the shortest path
13. S = set of datasets that P_{min} traversed;   //Except d_s and d_e
14. $SCR = (\Sigma_{d_i \in DDG} CostR_i)_s$;
15. Return S, SCR;

Figure 5.2 Pseudo-code of linear CTT-SP algorithm for benchmarking.

shows the pseudo-code of the linear CTT-SP algorithm. To construct the CTT, we first create the cost edges (lines 1−3), and then calculate their weights (lines 4−11). Next, we use the Dijkstra algorithm to find the SP (line 12) and return the MCSS and the minimum cost benchmark (lines 13−15).

From the pseudo-code in Figure 5.2, we can clearly see that for a linear DDG with n data sets, we have to add a magnitude of n^2 edges to construct the CTT (line 3 with two nested loops in lines 1−2), and for the longest edge, the time complexity of calculating its weight is also $O(n^2)$ (lines 5−11 with two nested loops), so a total of $O(n^4)$. Next, the Dijkstra algorithm (line 12) has the known time complexity of $O(n^2)$. Hence the linear CTT-SP algorithm has a worst-case time complexity of $O(n^4)$.

5.1.2   Minimum Cost Benchmarking Algorithm for DDG with One Block

Linear DDG is a special case of general DDGs. In the real world, application data sets generated in the cloud may have complex relationships, such that different data sets may be generated from a single data set by different operations, and different data sets may be used together to generate one data set. In other words, DDG may have branches, where the linear CTT-SP algorithm introduced in Section 5.1.1 cannot be directly applied. This is because current CTT can only be constructed on linear DDG, which means that the data sets in a DDG must be totally ordered. In this sub-section, we discuss how to find the MCSS of the DDG that has a sub-branch within one block for benchmarking.

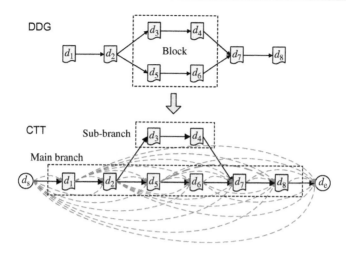

Figure 5.3 An example of constructing CTT for DDG with one block.

5.1.2.1 Constructing CTT for DDG with One Block

First, we introduce the concept of 'block' in DDG. Block is a set of sub-branches in the DDG that splits from a common data set and merges into another common data set. We denote the block as B. Figure 5.3 shows a DDG with a simple block $B = \{d_3, d_4, d_5, d_6\}$, we will use it as the example to illustrate the construction of CTT in our new algorithm.

To construct the CTT, we need the data sets in DDG to be totally ordered. Hence for the DDG with one block, we only choose one branch to construct the CTT, as shown is Figure 5.3. We call the linear data sets which are chosen to construct the CTT 'main branch', denoted as MB, and call the rest of data sets 'sub-branch(es)', denoted as SB. For example, in the DDG shown in Figure 5.3, MB = $\{d_1, d_2, d_5, d_6, d_7, d_8\}$ and $SB = \{d_3, d_4\}$. Due to the existence of the block, the edges can be classified into four categories. The definition of this classification is as follows:

- **In-block edge:** $e < d_i, d_j >$ is an in-block edge meaning that the edge starts from d_i, which is a data set outside of the block, and points to d_j, which is a data set in the block, such as $e < d_2, d_5 >$, $e < d_1, d_6 >$ in Figure 5.3. Formally, we define $e < d_i, d_j >$ as an in-block edge, where:

$$\exists d_k \in DDG \wedge d_i \to d_k \wedge d_j \leftrightarrow d_k$$

- **Out-block edge:** $e < d_i, d_j >$ is an out-block edge meaning that the edge starts from d_i, which is a data set in the block, and points to d_j, which is a data set outside of the block, such as $e < d_6, d_7 >$, $e < d_5, d_8 >$ in Figure 5.3. Formally, we define $e < d_i, d_j >$ as an out-block edge, where:

$$\exists d_k \in DDG \wedge d_i \leftrightarrow d_k \wedge d_k \to d_j$$

- **Over-block edge:** $e<d_i, d_j>$ is an over-block edge meaning that the edge crosses over the block, where d_i is a data set preceding the block, d_j is a data set succeeding the block, such as $e<d_2, d_7>$, $e<d_1, d_8>$ in Figure 5.3. Formally, we define $e<d_i, d_j>$ as an over-block edge, where:

$$\exists d_k, d_h \in DDG \wedge d_h \leftrightarrow d_k \wedge d_i \rightarrow d_h \rightarrow d_j \wedge d_i \rightarrow d_k \rightarrow d_j$$

- **Ordinary edge:** $e<d_i, d_j>$ is an ordinary edge meaning that data sets between d_i and d_j are totally ordered, such as $e<d_s, d_2>$, $e<d_5, d_6>$, $e<d_7, d_8>$ in Figure 5.3. Formally, we define $e<d_i, d_j>$ as an ordinary edge, where:

$$\neg \exists d_k \in DDG \wedge ((d_i \rightarrow d_k \wedge d_k \leftrightarrow d_j) \vee (d_i \leftrightarrow d_k \wedge d_k \rightarrow d_j)$$
$$\vee (d_h \in DDG \wedge d_h \leftrightarrow d_k \wedge d_i \rightarrow d_h \rightarrow d_j \wedge d_i \rightarrow d_k \rightarrow d_j))$$

5.1.2.2   Setting Weights to Different Types of Edges

The essence of the CTT-SP algorithm is the rules for setting weights to the cost edges. In order to set weights to different types of edges in the DDG with one block, we need to introduce an important corollary of Theorem 5.1.

Corollary 5.1 *During the process of finding the SP, for every data set d_f that is discovered by the Dijkstra algorithm, we have a path $P_{min}<d_s, d_f>$ from d_s to d_f and a set of data sets S_f that $P_{min}<d_s, d_f>$ traverses. S_f is the MCSS of the sub-DDG segment*

$$\{d_i | d_i \in DDG \wedge d_s \rightarrow d_i \rightarrow d_f\}.$$

In the CTT-SP algorithm, the rules for setting weights to the edges guarantee that the paths from the start data set d_s to every data set d_i in the CTT represent the storage strategies of the data sets $\{d_k | d_k \in DDG \wedge d_s \rightarrow d_k \rightarrow d_i\}$, and Corollary 5.1 further indicates that the SP represent the MCSS. As defined in Section 5.1.1, the weight of the edge $e<d_i, d_j>$ is the sum of cost rates of d_j and the data sets between d_i and d_j, supposing that only d_i and d_j are stored and the rest of data sets between d_i and d_j are all deleted. In the DDG with one block, this rule is still applicable to the ordinary edges and in-block edges.

However, if $e<d_i, d_j>$ is an out-block edge or over-block edge, Eq. (5.1) in Section 5.1.1 is not applicable for calculating its weight anymore because of the following:

1. Due to the existence of the block, the data sets succeeding the block may have more than one data sets in their *provSets*. The generation of these data sets needs not only d_i but also the stored provenance data sets from the other sub-branches of the block. For example, according to Eq. (5.1) in Section 5.1.1, the weight of the out-block edge $e<d_5, d_8>$ in Figure 5.3 is:

$$\omega<d_5, d_8> = y_8 + genCost(d_6) * v_6 + genCost(d_7) * v_7$$

where if we want to calculate genCost(d_7), we also have to know the storage statuses of d_3 and d_4. The same problem also exists when calculating the weights of the over-block edges. Hence to calculate the weights of out-block and over-block edges, we have to know the storage strategies of all the sub-branches in the block.

2. The path from d_s to d_j cannot represent the storage strategy of all the data sets $\{d_k | d_k \in \text{DDG} \wedge d_s \rightarrow d_k \rightarrow d_j\}$. If we use the same method in Section 5.1.1 to set the weight of $e < d_i, d_j>$, the path that contains $e < d_i, d_j>$ in the CTT can only represent the storage strategy of data sets in the main branch, where the sub-branches are not represented. For example, in Figure 5.3, the path from d_s to d_8 that contains the out-block edge $e < d_5, d_8>$ does not represent the storage statuses of data sets d_3 and d_4, and the length of the path also does not contain the cost rates of d_3 and d_4, if we use the method in Section 5.1.1 to calculate the weights of the edges. Hence to maintain the mapping between the paths and the storage strategies, the weights of out-block and over-block edges should contain the minimum cost rates of the data sets in the sub-branches of the block.

Based on the reasons above, if $e < d_i, d_j>$ is an out-block edge or over-block edge, we define its weight as:

$$\omega < d_i, d_j> = y_j + \sum_{\{d_k | d_k \in \text{MB} \wedge d_i \rightarrow d_k \rightarrow d_j\}} (genCost(d_k) * v_k) + \left(\sum_{\{d_h | d_h \in \text{SB}\}} CostR_h \right)_{S'}$$
(5.2)

In Eq. (5.2), $\left(\sum_{\{d_h | d_h \in \text{SB}\}} CostR_h \right)_{S'}$ is the sum of cost rates of the data sets that are in the sub-branches of the block, where S' is the MCSS of the sub-branches. This equation guarantees that the length of the SP with an out-block edge or over-block edge still equals the minimum cost rate of the data sets, which is:

$$P_{\min} < d_s, d_j> = \left(\sum_{\{d_k | d_k \in \text{DDG} \wedge d_s \rightarrow d_k \rightarrow d_j\}} CostR_k \right)_{S'}$$

Hence to calculate the weights of out-block and over-block edges, we have to find the MCSS of the data sets that are in the sub-branches of the block. For example, the weight of the edge $e < d_5, d_8>$ in Figure 5.3 is:

$$\omega < d_5, d_8> = y_8 + genCost(d_6) * v_6 + genCost(d_7) * v_7 + (CostR_3 + CostR_4)_{S'}$$

where we have to find the MCSS of data sets d_3 and d_4.

However, for any sub-branch, the MCSS is dependent on the storage status of the data sets preceding and succeeding the block (i.e. stored adjacent predecessor and successor of the sub-branches).

If $e < d_i, d_j >$ is an over-block edge, according to the rules of setting weight, d_i and d_j are stored data sets, and the data sets between d_i and d_j in the main branch, $\{d_k | d_k \in MB \wedge d_i \to d_k \to d_j\}$, are deleted. Hence d_i and d_j are the stored adjacent predecessor and successor of the sub-branch. If the rest of the data sets within the block form a linear DDG, we can use the linear CTT-SP algorithm introduced in Section 5.1.1 to find its MCSS, where in the first step we have to use d_i and d_j as the start and end data sets. For example, to calculate the weight of over-block edge $e < d_1, d_8 >$ in Figure 5.3, we have to find the MCSS S' of sub-branch $\{d_3, d_4\}$ by the linear CTT-SP algorithm, given that d_1 is the start data set and d_8 is the end data set. Otherwise, if the rest of data sets within the block do not form a linear DDG, we have to recursively call the CTT-SP algorithm to find the MCSS of sub-branches, which will be introduced in Section 5.1.3. Hence the weight of an over-block edge can be calculated.

If $e < d_i, d_j >$ is an out-block edge, we only know the stored adjacent successor of the sub-branches is d_j. However, the MCSS of the sub-branches is also dependent on the stored adjacent predecessor, which is unknown for an out-block edge. Hence given different stored adjacent predecessors, the weight of an out-block edge would be different. For example, to calculate the weight of out-block edge $e < d_5, d_8 >$ in Figure 5.3, we need to find the MCSS S' of the sub-branch $\{d_3, d_4\}$, where we only know the stored adjacent successor d_8. However, S' may be different depending on the storage statuses of d_1 and d_2. Hence we have to create multiple CTTs for the DDG with a block in order to calculate the weights of out-block edges in different situations, as detailed next.

5.1.2.3   Steps of Finding MCSS for DDG with One Sub-Branch in One Block

In this sub-section, we extend the linear CTT-SP algorithm to find its MCSS for DDG with one sub-branch in the block. As discussed in Section 5.1.2.2, depending on different stored preceding data sets of the block, the weight of an out-block edge may be different. Hence multiple CTTs are needed to represent these different situations, and the MCSS is the SP among all the CTTs.

To find the MCSS for a DDG with one sub-branch in the block, we need the following two theorems.

Theorem 5.2 *The selection of main branch in the* DDG *to construct* CTT *has no impact on finding the* MCSS.

Theorem 5.3 *The Dijkstra algorithm is still applicable to find the* MCSS *of the* DDG *with one block.*

Based on these two theorems, we design the algorithm for finding the MCSS for the DDG with one block. The main steps are as follows.

Step 1: Construct the initial CTT of the DDG. According to Theorem 5.2, we choose an arbitrary branch in the DDG as the main branch and add cost edges to construct the CTT. In the CTT, for the ordinary edges and in-block edges, we set their weights based on

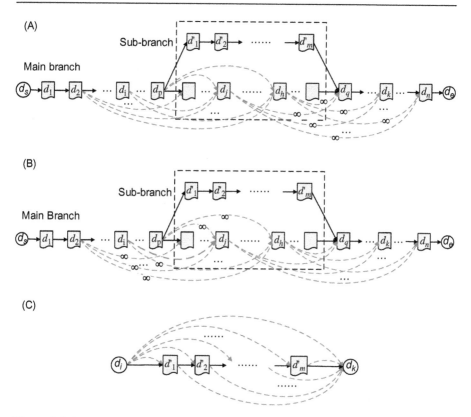

Figure 5.4 CTTs for DDG with one block. (A) Initial CTT for DDG; (B) CTT(e < di,dj>) for in-block edge $e < di,dj>$; (C) CTT created for the sub-branch.

Eq. (5.1) in Section 5.1.1. For the over-block edges, we set their weights according to Eq. (5.2) by calling the linear CTT-SP algorithm to find the MCSS of the sub-branch, which is introduced in Section 5.1.2.2. For the out-block edges, we initialise their weights as infinity. The initial CTT is shown in Figure 5.4A. We create a CTT set and add the initial CTT to it.

Step 2: Based on Theorem 5.3, start the Dijkstra algorithm to find the SP from d_s to d_e, which applies to all CTTs in the CTT set. We use F to denote the set of data sets discovered by the Dijkstra algorithm. When a new edge $e < d_i, d_j >$ is discovered, we first add d_j to F, and then check whether $e < d_i, d_j >$ is an in-block edge or not. If not, we continue to find the next edge by the Dijkstra algorithm until d_e is reached, which would terminate the algorithm. If $e < d_i, d_j >$ is an in-block edge, create a new CTT (see Steps 2.1–2.3 next) because whenever an in-block edge is discovered, a stored adjacent predecessor of the sub-branch is identified, and this data set will be used in calculating the weights of out-block edges. Then we continue the Dijkstra algorithm to find the next edge.

Step 2.1: In the case where in-block edge $e < d_i, d_j >$ is discovered, based on the current CTT, create CTT($e < d_i, d_j >$) as shown in Figure 5.4B. First, we copy all the information of the current CTT to new CTT($e < d_i, d_j >$). Second, we update the weights of all the in-block edges in CTT($e < d_i, d_j >$) as infinity, except $e < d_i, d_j >$. This guarantees that data set d_i is the stored adjacent predecessor of the sub-branch in all the paths of CTT($e < d_i, d_j >$). Third, we update the weights of all the out-block edges in CTT($e < d_i, d_j >$) as described next.

Step 2.2: Calculate the weight of an out-block edge $e < d_h, d_k >$ in CTT($e < d_i, d_j >$). As discussed in Section 5.1.2.2, to calculate the weight of $e < d_h, d_k >$ according to Eq. (5.2), we have to find the MCSS of the sub-branch in the block. From Figure 5.4B we can see that the sub-branch is $\{d'_1, d'_2, \ldots, d'_m\}$, which is a linear DDG. We can find its MCSS by using the linear CTT-SP algorithm described in Section 5.1.1, given that d_i is the start data set and d_k is the end data set. The CTT created for the sub-branch is shown in Figure 5.4C.

Step 2.3: Add new CTT($e < d_i, d_j >$) to the CTT set.

5.1.3 Minimum Cost Benchmarking Algorithm for General DDG

In real-world applications, the structure of DDG could be complex, i.e. there may exist more than one block in a DDG. However, to find the MCSS of a general DDG, no matter how complex the DDG's structure is, we can deduce the calculation process to the linear DDG situations by recursively calling the algorithm introduced in Section 5.1.2. In this sub-section we present the general CTT-SP algorithm for benchmarking. First, we discuss different situations of the algorithm for a general DDG, and then we give the pseudo-code for finding the MCSS for general DDG.

5.1.3.1 General CTT-SP Algorithm for Different Situations

The complex structure of a DDG can be viewed as a combination of many blocks. Following the algorithm steps introduced in Section 5.1.2.3, we choose an arbitrary branch from the start data set d_s to the end data set d_e as the main branch to construct the initial CTT and create multiple CTTs for different in-block edges discovered by the Dijkstra algorithm. In the process of calculating the weights of out-block and over-block edges, there are two new situations for finding the MCSS of the sub-branches.

1. The sub-branches may have more than one stored adjacent predecessor. For example, $e < d_i, d_j >$ in Figure 5.5 is an out-block edge of block B_1, and also an in-block edge of block B_2. In the algorithm, if edge $e < d_i, d_j >$ is found by the Dijkstra algorithm, we create a new CTT($e < d_i, d_j >$) from the current CTT, since $e < d_i, d_j >$ is an in-block edge of block B_2. To calculate the weights of out-block edges in CTT($e < d_i, d_j >$), for example $e < d_h, d_k >$ in Figure 5.5, we need to find the MCSS of the sub-branch $\{d_1, d_2, \ldots, d'_m\}$ of block B_2. However, because $e < d_i, d_j >$ is also an out-block edge of B_1, d_i is not the only data set in *provSet* of d_1'. To calculate the generation cost of d_1, we need to find its stored provenance data sets from sub-branch Br_1 of block B_1.

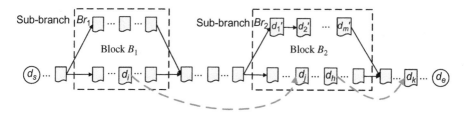

Figure 5.5 Sub-branch with more than one stored adjacent predecessor.

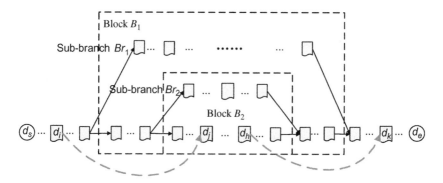

Figure 5.6 Sub-branch with branches.

2. The sub-branches are a general DDG which also has branches. In this situation, we need to recursively call the general CTT-SP algorithm to find its MCSS. For example, $e < d_i$, $d_j >$ in Figure 5.6 is an in-block edge of blocks B_1 and B_2. If $e < d_i$, $d_j >$ is selected by the algorithm, we need to create a new CTT($e < d_i$, $d_j >$). To calculate the weight of $e < d_h$, $d_k >$ in Figure 5.6, which is an out-block edge of both B_1 and B_2, we need to find the MCSS of the sub-branches Br_1 and Br_2. Hence we have to recursively call the general CTT-SP algorithm for the DDG $Br_1 \cup Br_2$, given the start data set d_i and the end data set d_k.

Hence given a general DDG, its structure can be viewed as a combination of many blocks. By recursively calling the general CTT-SP algorithm for the sub-branches, we can eventually find the MCSS of the whole DDG. Figure 5.7 shows an example of general DDG. To create CTT($e < d_i$, $d_j >$), we need to calculate the weights of all the out-block edges. For example, for an out-block edge $e < d_h$, $d_k >$, we need to further find the MCSS of the sub-branches $\{d_u | d_u \in DDG \wedge d_u \rightarrow d_k \wedge d_u \leftrightarrow d_j \wedge d_u \leftrightarrow d_h\}$, as shown in Figure 5.7, given the start data set d_i and the end data set d_k.

5.1.3.2 Pseudo-Code of General CTT-SP Algorithm

Figure 5.8 shows the pseudo-code of the general CTT-SP algorithm. At the beginning, we choose an arbitrary branch from d_s to d_e as the main branch to construct

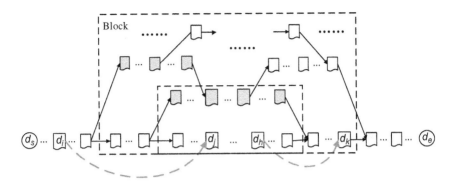

Figure 5.7 CTT for general DDG.

the initial CTT (lines 1—21), where we need to recursively call the general CTT-SP algorithm in calculating the weights for over-block edges (lines 11—14). Then we start the Dijkstra algorithm (lines 22—50). Whenever an in-block edge is found, we construct a new CTT with the following steps. First, we create a copy of the current CTT, in which the in-block edge is found (line 31). Next, we update the weights of edges: lines 32—34 are for updating the weights of in-block edges and lines 35—49 are for updating the weights of out-block edges. If the sub-branch is a linear DDG, we call the linear CTT-SP algorithm described in Figure 5.2, otherwise we recursively call the general CTT-SP algorithm (lines 39—42). At last, we add the new CTT to the CTTSet (line 50) and continue the Dijkstra algorithm to find the next edge. When the end data set d_e is reached, the algorithm ends with the MCSS and the minimum cost benchmark returned (lines 51—53).

From the pseudo-code in Figure 5.8, we can see that recursive calls (line 14 and line 42) exist in the general CTT-SP algorithm, which makes the algorithm's complexity highly dependent on the structure of DDG. Next, we analyse the worst-case scenario of the algorithm and show that the time complexity is polynomial.

In Figure 5.8, pseudo-code lines 1—21 are for constructing one CTT, i.e. the initial CTT. From pseudo-code lines 24—50 of the general CTT-SP algorithm, many CTTs are created for the DDG during the deployment of the Dijkstra algorithm, which determine the algorithm's computation complexity. The maximum number of the created CTTs is smaller than the number of data sets in the main branch, which is in the magnitude of n. Hence if we denote the time complexity of the general CTT-SP algorithm as $F_l(n)$, we have the recursive equation as follows:

$$\begin{cases} F_0(n) = O(n^4) \\ F_r(n) = n^3 * (F_{r-1}(n_{(r-1)}) + n^2), \quad r > 0 \end{cases} \tag{5.3}$$

In Eq. (5.3), n is the number of data sets in the DDG, $n_{(r-1)}$ is the number of data sets in the sub-branches, and r is the maximum level of the recursive calls, especially $F_0(n)$ denotes the situation of linear DDG, where the linear CTT-SP algorithm needs to be called (i.e. pseudo-code in Figure 5.2).

Algorithm:	General_CTT-SP	
Input:	start dataset d_s; end dataset d_e;	
	a general DDG;	//Include d_s and d_e
Output:	S; SCR;	//MCSS of the DDG and the minimum cost benchmark

01. Get a main branch MB from DDG;
02. **for** (every dataset d_i in MB)   //Create initial CTT
03.   **for** (every dataset d_j, where $d_j \in MB \wedge d_i \to d_j$)
04.   Create $e < d_i, d_j >$;   //Create an edge
05.   **if** ($\exists d_k \in DDG \wedge d_i \leftrightarrow d_k \wedge d_k \to d_j$)   //e is an out-block edge
06.   Set $\omega < d_i, d_j >= \infty$;
07.   **else**   //Calculate the weight of the edge
08. $weight = 0$;
09.   **if** ($\exists d_k \notin MB \wedge d_i \to d_k \to d_j$)   //e is an over-block edge
10. $SB = \{d_k | d_k \notin MB \wedge d_i \to d_k \to d_j\}$;   //Get the sub-branches SB
11.   **if** (SB is linear)   //Find the minimum cost storage strategy of SB
12. $S' = $ Linear_CTT-SP(d_i, d_j, SB);
13.   **else**
14. $S' = $ General_CTT-SP(d_i, d_j, SB);
15. $weight = weight + \left(\sum_{d_i \in SB} CostR_i\right)_{S'}$;
16.   **for** (every dataset d_k, where $d_k \in MB \wedge d_i \to d_k \to d_j$)   //Datasets in main branch
17. $genCost = 0$;
18.   **for** (every dataset d_h, where $d_h \in MB \wedge d_i \to d_h \to d_k$)
19. $genCost = genCost + x_h$;
20. $weight = weight + \left(x_k + genCost\right) * v_k$;   //Sum of generation cost rate s
21.   Set $\omega < d_i, d_j >= weight + y_j$;   //Set weight to the edge
22. $CTTSet = \{CTT_{ini}\}$;   //Set of all the created CTTs
23. $F = \{\emptyset\}$;   //Set of datasets discovered by Dijkstra algorithm
24. **while** (d_e is not in F)
25.   **for** (every CTT in $CTTSet$)   //Find the next edge for the shortest path
26.   Find the next edge by Dijkstra algorithm;
27.   Get the current shortest path in all the $CTTs$, which is with the edge $e < d_i, d_j >\in CTT'$
28.   Add d_j to F;
29.   **if** ($\exists d_b \in DDG \wedge d_i \to d_b \wedge d_j \leftrightarrow d_b$)   //e is an in-block edge
30. $BSet = \{B_p | B_p \subset DDG \wedge d_i \notin B_p \wedge d_j \in B_p\}$;   //Blocks that contains d_j but not d_i
31.   Create a copy of CTT' denoted as $CTT(e<d_i, d_j>)$;   //Create a new CTT
32.   **for** (every $B_p \in BSet$)   //Update the weights of the in -block edges
33.   **for** (every $e < d_r, d_t >\neq e < d_i, d_j >$ where $d_r \notin B_p \wedge d_t \in B_p$)
34.   Set $\omega < d_r, d_t >= \infty$;
35.   **for** (every $B_p \in BSet$)   //Update the weights of out -block edges
36.   **for** (every $e < d_h, d_k >$ where $d_h \in B_p \wedge d_j \to d_h \wedge d_k \notin B_p$)
37. $weight = 0$;
38. $SB = \{d_p | d_p \in DDG \wedge d_i \to d_p \to d_k \wedge d_j \leftrightarrow d_p \wedge d_p \leftrightarrow d_h\}$; //Get the sub-branches
39.   **if** (SB is linear)   //Find the minimum cost storage strategy of SB
40. $S' = $ Linear_CTT-SP(d_i, d_k, SB);
41.   **else**
42. $S' = $ General_CTT-SP(d_i, d_k, SB);
43. $weight = \left(\sum_{d_i \in SB} CostR_i\right)_{S'}$;
44.   **for** (every dataset d_l, where $d_l \in MB \wedge d_h \to d_l \to d_k$) //Datasets in main branch
45. $genCost = 0$;
46.   **for** (every dataset d_o, where $d_o \in MB \wedge d_h \to d_o \to d_l$)
47. $genCost = genCost + x_o$;
48. $weight = weight + \left(x_l + genCost\right) * v_l$;   //Sum of generation cost rate
49.   Set $\omega < d_h, d_k >= weight + y_k$;   //Set weight to the out -block edge
50.   Add $CTT(e<d_i, d_j>)$ to $CTTSet$;
51. $S = $ set of datasets that the shortest path from d_s to d_e has traversed;
52. $SCR = \left(\sum_{d_i \in DDG} CostR_i\right)$;
53. Return S, SCR;

Figure 5.8 Pseudo-code of general CTT-SP algorithm for benchmarking.

Intuitively, in Eq. (5.3), $F_r(n)$ seems to have an exponential complexity (i.e. NP-hard) depending on the level of recursive calls. However, in our scenario, $F_r(n)$ is polynomial because the recursive call is to find the MCSS of given sub-branches in DDG which has a limited solution space. Hence we can use the iterative method [64] to solve the recursive equation and derive the computation complexity of the general CTT-SP algorithm.

If we assume that we have already found the MCSSs for all sub-branches (which means without taking the impact of recursive calls into account), the general CTT-SP algorithm has a time complexity of $O(n^5)$, because there are five nested loops in the pseudo-code in Figure 5.8 (lines 24, 35, 36, 44, 46). Formally, we can transform Eq. (5.3) to the following:

$$
\begin{aligned}
F_r(n) &= n^3 * (O(1) + n^2) + f_{\text{rec}}(F_{r-1}(n_{(r-1)})) \\
&= O(n^5) + f_{\text{rec}}(F_{r-1}(n_{(r-1)}))
\end{aligned}
\tag{5.4}
$$

In Eq. (5.4), function f_{rec} denotes the complexity of recursive calls, i.e. calculating the minimum cost storage strategies of all sub-branches. Next, we analyse the complexity of recursive calls.

For a sub-branch of a general DDG, given a different start data set and end data set, its MCSS may be different. Figure 5.9 shows a sub-branch of DDG with w data sets. We assume that direct predecessors of d_1 and direct successors of d_w are all stored, and then we can find a MCSS of the sub-branch. We denote the first stored data set as d_u and the last stored data set as d_v in the strategy, which is shown in Figure 5.9. If the adjacent stored predecessors of d_1 are changed, the MCSS may be different as well. Since the generation cost of d_1 is larger than storing the direct predecessors, the first stored data set in the new strategy must be one of the data sets from d_1 to d_u. Similarly, if the adjacent stored successors of d_w are changed, the last stored data set in the new strategy must be one of the data sets from d_v to d_w. Hence given different start and end data sets, a sub-branch of DDG has at most $u \times (w - v)$ different minimum cost storage strategies, which are in the magnitude of w^2. Hence we have the conclusion that for any sub-branches of DDG with w data sets, there are at most w^2 different minimum cost storage strategies, given different start and end data sets. Hence given any sub-branches in DDG at any level of recursive calls, say level h, we have the time complexity $F_h(w) \times w^2$ for finding all the possible minimum cost storage strategies.

Figure 5.9 A sub-branch in DDG.

If we assume that there are m different sub-branches of recursive calls at level h for which we have to find the minimum cost storage strategies, we have the complexity of recursive calls at this level as follows:

$$f_{\text{rec}}(F_h(n_h)) \leq \sum_{i=1}^{m}(F_h(n_{h,i}) * n_{h,i}^2) \tag{5.5}$$

With Eq. (5.5), we can further transform Eq. (5.4) and iteratively derive the time complexity of the general CTT-SP algorithm.

Therefore the entire iteration process from Eq. (5.3) is shown as follows:

$$
\begin{aligned}
F_r(n) &= n^3 * (F_{r-1}(n_{(r-1)}) + n^2) \\
&= O(n^5) + f_{\text{rec}}(F_{r-1}(n_{(r-1)})) \quad //\text{from Eq. (5.4)} \\
&\leq O(n^5) + \sum_{i=1}^{m_{r-1}}(F_{r-1}(n_{(r-1),i}) * n_{(r-1),i}^2) \quad //\text{from Eq. (5.5)} \\
&= O(n^5) + \sum_{i=1}^{m_{r-1}}(n_{(r-1),i}^3 * (F_{r-2}(n_{(r-2),i}) + n_{(r-1),i}^2) * n_{(r-1),i}^2) \quad //\text{recursion} \\
&\leq O(n^5) + \sum_{i=1}^{m_{r-1}}(O((n_{(r-1),i})^5) * n_{(r-1),i}^2) \\
&\quad + \sum_{i=1}^{m_{r-2}}(F_{r-2}(n_{(r-2),i}) * n_{(r-2),i}^2) \quad //\text{from Eqs. (5.4) and (5.5)} \\
&\leq O(n^5) + \sum_{i=1}^{m_{r-1}}(O((n_{(r-1),i})^5) * n_{(r-1),i}^2) + \ldots + \sum_{i=1}^{m_0}(F_0(n_{0,i}) * n_{0,i}^2) \quad //\text{iteration} \\
&= O(n^5) + \sum_{j=r-1}^{1}\left(\sum_{i=1}^{m_j}(O((n_{j,i})^5) * n_{j,i}^2)\right) + \sum_{i=1}^{m_0}(O(n_{0,i}^4) * n_{0,i}^2) \quad //F_0(n) = O(n^4) \\
&\leq r * m * O(n^5) * n^2 \quad //m = \max_{i=0}^{j}(m_i) \\
&\leq O(n^9) \quad //r < n, \ m < n
\end{aligned}
$$

Hence the worst-case time complexity of the general CTT-SP algorithm is $O(n^9)$.

Based on the complexity analysis, we can see that the general CTT-SP algorithm provides a benchmarking approach for a seemingly NP-hard problem with a polynomial solution.

In Chapter 7, we will use experiment results to further demonstrate this on-demand benchmarking approach.

5.2 Dynamic On-the-Fly Minimum Cost Benchmarking Approach

In this section, we describe our novel on-the-fly minimum cost benchmarking approach in detail. The basic idea is that we divide the whole DDG into smaller linear DDG segments (DDG_LS) and create a partitioned solution space (PSS) for every segment. PSS saves all the possible MCSSs of the DDG segment, which are calculated by the CTT-SP algorithm. The minimum cost benchmark of the whole DDG can be calculated by merging the PSSs. Whenever new data sets are generated and/or existing data sets' usage frequencies are changed, the new benchmark can be dynamically located on the fly from the pre-calculated PSSs merely by calling the CTT-SP algorithm on the small local DDG segment for adjustment. Hence we can keep the minimum cost benchmark updated on the fly so that users' benchmarking requests can be instantly responded to.

5.2.1 PSS for a DDG_LS

PSS is the basis of our dynamic benchmarking approach. In this sub-section, we first explain the reason why there exists a solution space of MCSSs for a DDG_LS. Then we introduce some properties of the solution space and further investigate how the MCSSs are distributed in a PSS.

5.2.1.1 Different MCSSs of a DDG_LS in a Solution Space

Generally speaking, a DDG_LS would only have one MCSS for storing the data sets. However, due to different preceding and succeeding data sets' storage statuses, there would be different corresponding MCSSs — one for each status.

The CTT-SP algorithm can be utilised not only on independent DDGs but also on DDG_LSs, where the difference is the selection of start and end data sets for constructing the CTT. For an independent DDG, we add two virtual data sets d_s and d_e as start and end data sets to construct the CTT as shown in Figure 5.1. However, for the CTT of a DDG_LS, the start data set d_s is the nearest stored preceding data set to the DDG_LS, and the end data set d_e is the nearest stored succeeding data set to the DDG_LS. Figure 5.10 shows an example of CTT for a DDG_LS.

Hence given different start and end data sets, the MCSS of a DDG_LS may be different. This is because the deleted preceding data sets impact on the generation

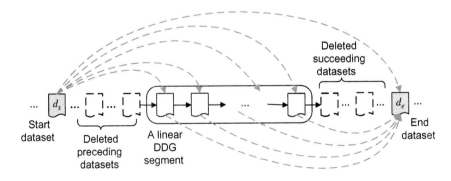

Figure 5.10 CTT for a DDG_LS.

cost of data sets in the DDG_LS and the generation of the deleted succeeding data sets need to use data sets in the DDG_LS.

Next, we analyse how the preceding and succeeding data sets of the DDG_LS impact on its MCSS.

Theorem 5.4 *For a DDG_LS, only the generation cost of its deleted preceding data sets and the usage frequencies of its deleted succeeding data sets impact on its MCSS.*

Based on Theorem 5.4, for a DDG_LS $\{d_1, d_2, \ldots, d_{nl}\}$, we introduce two definitions:

- $X = \sum_{\{i|d_i \in DDG \wedge d_s \to d_i \to d_1\}} x_i$ is the sum of preceding data sets generation costs of a DDG_LS, where d_i is a deleted preceding data set.
- $V = \sum_{\{j|d_j \in DDG \wedge d_{n_l} \to d_j \to d_e\}} v_j$ is the sum of succeeding data sets usage frequencies of a DDG_LS, where d_j is a deleted succeeding data set.

For different start and end data sets, the values of X and V are different, and the MCSS of the DDG_LS may also be different. In other words, given different X and V, there exist different MCSSs for storing the DDG_LS. We denote an MCSS as $S_{i,j}$, where d_i and d_j are the first and last stored data sets in the strategy, which could be any data sets in the DDG_LS. Conversely, any two data sets d_i and d_j in the DDG_LS may be the first and last stored data sets of an MCSS. Hence theoretically, the number of different MCSSs for a DDG_LS is in the magnitude of n_l^2, where n_l is the number of data sets in the DDG_LS.

5.2.1.2 Range of MCSSs' Cost Rates for a DDG_LS

Different MCSSs have different cost rates (i.e. SCR defined in Eq. (4.4) in Section 4.3) for storing the DDG_LS. Since DDG_LS is a segment of the whole DDG, the total cost rate of storing it includes not only its own cost rate but also the cost rate of generating the deleted preceding and succeeding data sets. Hence given any X and V, and the corresponding MCSS $S_{i,j}$, we denote the total cost rate of storing the DDG_LS $\{d_1, d_2, \ldots, d_{nl}\}$ as $TCR_{i,j}$, where:

$$TCR_{i,j} = X * \sum_{k=1}^{i-1} v_k + SCR_{i,j} + V * \sum_{k=j+1}^{n_l} x_k \qquad (5.6)$$

In Eq. (5.6), $SCR_{i,j}$ is the cost rate of storing the DDG_LS with the storage strategy $S_{i,j}$, assuming that the direct preceding and succeeding data sets of DDG_LS are stored. Formally:

$$SCR_{i,j} = \left(\sum_{d_k \in DDG\_LS} CostR_k \right)_{S_{i,j}} \qquad (5.7)$$

An important difference between $TCR_{i,j}$ and $SCR_{i,j}$ is that $TCR_{i,j}$ is a variable for a storage strategy depending on the value of X and V (see Eq. (5.6)), whereas $SCR_{i,j}$ is a constant for a specific storage strategy (see Eq. (5.7)).

For a DDG_LS, one extreme situation of $(X = 0, V = 0)$ means that the start and end data sets are the direct preceding and succeeding data sets of the DDG_LS. Hence we can deem the DDG_LS as an independent DDG and directly call the CTT-SP algorithm to find its MCSS. In this situation, MCSS $S_{u,v}$ found is the minimum $SCR_{u,v}$ for storing the DDG_LS among other MCSSs, where $TCR_{u,v} = SCR_{u,v}$. We denote $S_{u,v}$ as S_{min} and $SCR_{u,v}$ as SCR_{min}.

The other extreme situation is that the start and end data sets are very far from the current DDG_LS, i.e. $X > y_1/v_1$, $V > y_{nl}/x_{nl}$. Obviously, in this situation the first data set d_1 and the last data set d_{nl} in the DDG_LS should be stored. Hence we can deem d_1 and d_{nl} as the start and end data sets and call the CTT-SP algorithm for the data sets between d_1 and d_{nl}. The found strategy together with d_1 and d_{nl} form the MCSS of the DDG_LS in this situation denoted as $S_{1,nl}$, where we also have $TCR_{1,nl} = SCR_{1,nl}$. We denote $S_{1,nl}$ as S_{max} and $SCR_{1,nl}$ as SCR_{max}.

Theorem 5.5 *Given a DDG_LS $\{d_1, d_2, \ldots, d_{nl}\}$, $SCR_{min}$is the cost rate of MCSS $S_{u,v}$with $X = 0$, $V = 0$, and $SCR_{max}$is the cost rate of MCSS $S_{1,nl}$with $X > y_1/v_1$, $V > y_{nl}/x_{nl}$. Then we have $SCR_{min} < SCR_{i,j} < SCR_{max}$, where $SCR_{i,j}$is the cost rate of MCSS $S_{i,j}$with any given X and V.*

Figure 5.11 shows the MCSSs for a DDG_LS whose SCR values are in the valid range indicated in Theorem 5.5. We can further find all these strategies and save them in a strategy set, denoted as S_All. Figure 5.12 shows the pseudo-code for finding S_All. The essence of this algorithm is the utilisation of the CTT-SP algorithm. Given a DDG_LS $\{d_1, d_2, \ldots, d_{nl}\}$, we first create the CTT for it (line 1). Then (line 2), we call the Dijkstra algorithm on the CTT to find the SP from d_s to d_e which are the two virtual data sets added when creating the CTT. The corresponding MCSS $S_{u, v}$ is S_{min} with SCR_{min}, where d_u and d_v are the first and last stored data sets in this MCSS. Similarly, we find S_{max} with SCR_{max} (line 3). Next, we initialise S_All and S_{max} (lines 4−5) and go through all the possible positions of the first and last stored data sets to find the corresponding MCSSs (lines 6−9). We eliminate the MCSSs

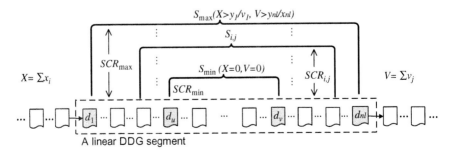

Figure 5.11 Different MCSSs for a DDG_LS.

with invalid SCR values according to Theorem 5.5 (line 10) and save the valid MCSSs in S_All (line 11).

The time complexity of creating the CTT is $O(n_l^4)$ (line 1) according to the CTT-SP algorithm [90], where n_l is the number of data sets in the DDG_LS. Next, the time complexity of finding all the possible MCSSs is n_l^2 (as indicated earlier at the end of Section 5.2.1.1) (lines 6–7) multiplying the time complexity of the Dijkstra algorithm, which is $O(n_l^2)$ (line 9). Hence the total time complexity of finding S_All is $O(n_l^4)$.

As discussed above, given any X and V, there exists one MCSS for storing the DDG_LS in the set of S_All. Hence we create a coordinate of X and V to represent the solution space of all possible MCSSs for a DDG_LS. Furthermore, we can calculate the distribution of the MCSSs in the solution space and call it PSS as described next.

5.2.1.3 Distribution of MCSSs in the PSS of a DDG_LS

We start by analysing the relationship of two MCSSs in the solution space. We assume that $S_{i,j}$ and $S_{i',j'}$ are two MCSSs in S_All of a DDG_LS $\{d_1, d_2, \ldots, d_{nl}\}$ and $SCR_{i,j} < SCR_{i',j'}.$ The border of $S_{i,j}$ and $S_{i',j'}$ in the solution space is that given particular X and V, the TCR of storing the DDG_LS with $S_{i,j}$ and $S_{i',j'}$ are equal. Hence we have:

$$TCR_{i,j} = TCR_{i',j'}$$
$$\Rightarrow X * \sum_{k=1}^{i-1} v_k + SCR_{i,j} + V * \sum_{k=j+1}^{n_l} x_k = X * \sum_{k=1}^{i'-1} v_k + SCR_{i',j'} + V * \sum_{k=j'+1}^{n_l} x_k$$
$$\Rightarrow \left(\sum_{k=1}^{i'-1} v_k - \sum_{k=1}^{i-1} v_k \right) * X + \left(\sum_{k=j'+1}^{n_l} x_k - \sum_{k=j+1}^{n_l} x_k \right) * V + (SCR_{i',j'} - SCR_{i,j}) = 0$$

$$(5.8)$$

Algorithm:	Find S_All
Input:	DDG_LS $\{d_1, d_2, \ldots d_{nl}\}$
Output:	S_All

```
01. Create CTT for DDG_S ;
02. S_min = S_u,v = Dijkstra_Path (CTT, d_s, d_e);
03. S_max = S_1,nl = Dijkstra_Path (CTT, d_1, d_nl);
04. Add S_min , S_max to S_All;
05. SCR_max = (Σ_{d_k∈DDG_S} CostR_k)_{S_max} ;
06. for ( i=1; i<=n_l; i++ )
07.     for ( j=1; j<=n_l; j++ )
08.         if (d_i → d_u ∨ d_v → d_j )
09.             S_i,j = Dijkstra_Path (CTT, d_i, d_j);
10.             if ((Σ_{d_k∈DDG_S} CostR_k)_{S_i,j} < SCR_max )
11.                 Add S_i,j to S_All;
12. Return S_All;          //Set of MCSSs with valid SCR
```

Figure 5.12 Pseudo-code of finding S_All.

From this equation we can see that the border of $S_{i,j}$ and $S_{i'j'}$ in the solution space is a straight line. Given different relationships of d_i and $d_{i'}$, d_j and $d_{j'}$, there are four different situations.

1. $d_{i'} \rightarrow d_i \wedge d_j \rightarrow d_{j'}$, as shown in Figure 5.13A, Eq. (5.8) can be further simplified to:

$$\left(\sum_{k=i'}^{i-1} v_k \right) * X + \left(\sum_{k=j+1}^{j'} x_k \right) * V - (SCR_{i',j'} - SCR_{i,j}) = 0 \qquad (5.9)$$

2. $d_i \rightarrow d_{i'} \wedge d_j \rightarrow d_{j'}$, as shown in Figure 5.13B, Eq. (5.8) can be further simplified to:

$$\left(\sum_{k=i}^{i'-1} v_k \right) * X - \left(\sum_{k=j+1}^{j'} x_k \right) * V + (SCR_{i',j'} - SCR_{i,j}) = 0 \qquad (5.10)$$

3. $d_{i'} \rightarrow d_i \wedge d_{j'} \rightarrow d_j$, as shown in Figure 5.13C, Eq. (5.8) can be further simplified to:

$$\left(\sum_{k=i'}^{i-1} v_k \right) * X - \left(\sum_{k=j'+1}^{j} x_k \right) * V - (SCR_{i',j'} - SCR_{i,j}) = 0 \qquad (5.11)$$

4. $d_i \rightarrow d_{i'} \wedge d_{j'} \rightarrow d_j$, as shown in Figure 5.13D, Eq. (5.8) can be further simplified to:

$$\left(\sum_{k=i}^{i'-1} v_k \right) * X + \left(\sum_{k=j'+1}^{j} x_k \right) * V + (SCR_{i',j'} - SCR_{i,j}) = 0$$

Since X and V are positive values, $S_{i',j'}$ can never be an eligible MCSS for the DDG_LS in the situation of Figure 5.13D. Hence we have a property of the MCSSs of a DDG_LS as follows:

$$(S_{i,j}, S_{i',j'} \in S\_All) \wedge (SCR_{i,j} \leq SCR_{i',j'}) \qquad \Rightarrow S_{i',j'} \notin PSS \qquad (5.12)$$
$$\wedge (d_i \rightarrow d_{i'} \wedge d_{j'} \rightarrow d_j)$$

Hence for any two MCSSs, we can find the partition line in the solution space which is one of the three equations listed above, namely Eqs. (5.9), (5.10), or (5.11). According to the property of Eq. (5.12), we can further eliminate some MCSSs from S_All, which should not be in the solution space. We refer the eligible MCSSs in S_All as S_ini, i.e. the initial input for calculating the solution space. From Figure 5.14, we can see that the time complexity of eliminating S_All is $O(n_s^2)$, where n_s is the number of MCSSs in S_All.

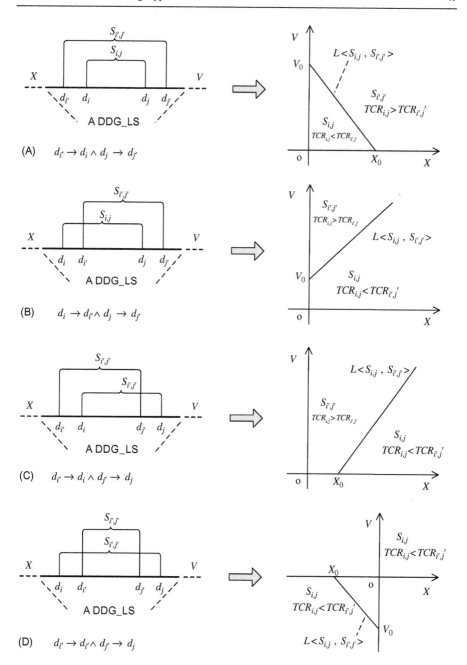

Figure 5.13 Examples of partition lines in a solution space.

Algorithm:	Eliminate S_All
Input:	S_All
Output:	S_ini

01. **for** (every $S_{i,j} \in S\_All$)
02.   **for** (every $S_{i',j'} \in S\_All \wedge SCR_{i,j} \leq SCR_{i',j}$)
03.   **if** ($d_i \rightarrow d_{i'} \wedge d_{j'} \rightarrow d_j$)
04.   Eliminate $S_{i',j'}$ from S_All;
05. Return the eliminated S_All as S_ini ;

Figure 5.14 Pseudo-code of eliminating S_All.

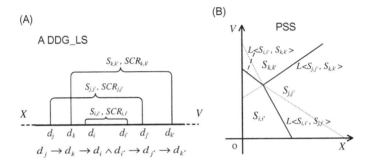

Figure 5.15 Example of Lemma 5.1. (A) Three MCSSs of a DDG_LS and (B) partition lines of the MCSSs.

From the above discussion, we can see that the solution space of a DDG_LS is partitioned by lines into different areas, which forms the PSS. In the PSS, every area represents an MCSS and the partition lines are the borders. Next, we describe our algorithms that can precisely calculate the PSS.

5.2.2 Algorithms for Calculating PSS of a DDG_LS

In a solution space, the MCSS of a DDG_LS changes from S_{min} to S_{max} as long as X and V increase. Given MCSS set S_ini, we calculate the partition line of every two adjacent strategies from S_{min} to S_{max}, and gradually partition the solution space. Finally, we derive a PSS, which includes all the possible MCSSs of the DDG_LS. In order to calculate the PSS for a DDG_LS, we need to introduce the following lemma.

Lemma 5.1 *In the PSS of a DDG_LS, for three MCSSs, if any two of them are adjacent to each other, then the three partition lines between every two MCSSs intersect at one point.*

In the statement of Lemma 5.1, two MCSSs are adjacent, meaning that the corresponding areas of the two MCSSs in the PSS are adjacent. Figure 5.15 shows an example of Lemma 5.1. We assume that $S_{i,i'}$, $S_{j,j'}$ and $S_{k,k'}$ be three MCSSs, where

$SCR_{i,i'} < SCR_{j,j'} < SCR_{k,k'}$ as shown in Figure 5.15A, and any two of $S_{i,i'}$, $S_{j,j'}$, $S_{k,k'}$ are adjacent as shown in Figure 5.15B. Based on the positions of the first and last stored data sets, we calculate the three partition lines as follows:

$$L < S_{i,i'}, S_{j,j'} > : \left(\sum_{h=j}^{i-1} v_h \right) * X + \left(\sum_{h=i'+1}^{j'} x_h \right) * V = SCR_{j,j'} - SCR_{i,i'}$$

$$L < S_{i,i'}, S_{k,k'} > : \left(\sum_{h=k}^{i-1} v_h \right) * X + \left(\sum_{h=i'+1}^{k'} x_h \right) * V = SCR_{k,k'} - SCR_{i,i'}$$

$$L < S_{j,j'}, S_{k,k'} > : - \left(\sum_{h=j}^{k-1} v_h \right) * X + \left(\sum_{h=j'+1}^{k'} x_h \right) * V = SCR_{k,k'} - SCR_{j,j'}$$

According to Lemma 5.1, these three lines intersect at one point in the PSS as shown in Figure 5.15B.

Based on Lemma 5.1, we design the algorithm to calculate the PSS for a DDG_LS. The main steps in the pseudo-code of this algorithm are shown in Figure 5.16.

As shown in Figure 5.16, the algorithm input is S_ini, which contains the possible MCSSs of a DDG_LS, and the output is the DDG_LS's PSS, which is a set of partition lines with start and end points in the solution space. The basic idea of the algorithm is to add the MCSSs to the PSS one by one from S_{min} to S_{max}, which contains three main steps:

- **Step 1**: initialisation and preparation (lines 1−4). First, we order the MCSSs in S_ini by their SCRs and save them in an ascending array list $[S_{min}, S_1, \ldots, S_{max}]$. Then we calculate the first partition line $L < S_{min}, S_1 >$ and its intercepts with the X and V axes, denoted as X_1 and V_1. Next, we create two ordered array lists X[] and V[] to store the intercepts of the partition lines with the X and V axes respectively. When we add an MCSS to the PSS, X[] and V[] are used to find the first MCSS in the PSS that we start calculating the partition lines. Last, we initialise the PSS with X and V axes, and add $L < S_{min}, S_1 >$ to it.
- **Step 2**: calculation of partition lines for an MCSS (lines 5−20). In this step, we start adding the MCSSs (i.e. $[S_{min}, S_1, \ldots, S_{max}]$) to the PSS.one by one (line 5). To add MCSS S_i to the PSS, first we need to find an adjacent MCSS to it in the PSS, based on which we start calculating the partition lines. To find an adjacent MCSS to S_i, we only need to calculate partition line $L < S_{min}, S_i >$ and insert intercepts X_i and V_i to X[] and V[] (lines 6−7). Adjacent MCSS S' is the corresponding MCSS of the first intercept that is smaller than X_i in X[] or V_i in V[]. Next, we add S_i to the PSS and start by calculating the partition line of S_i and S' (line 10). As S' is an existing MCSS in the PSS which represents some areas in the solution space, partition line $L < S', S_i >$ intersects with the border of S' and new MCSS S_i partially overlaps with existing MCSS S. Hence we find the border-lines of S' (line 11) and calculate the intersections of $L < S', S_i >$ (lines 12−13). We also need to save the intersections (lines 14−17), where set av_point saves all the intersections that will be used in the next step and stack v_point saves the intersections, which indicate the next MCSS that S_i partitions. Next, we add partition line $L < S', S_i >$ as well as the endpoints (i.e. the intersections just calculated) to the PSS (line 18), and then, by popping an intersection from v_point (line 19), we find the next MCSS to partition with S_i which

Algorithm: **Calculate** *PSS*
Input: *S_ini*   //the MCSSs set
Output: *PSS*   //with partition lines

01. Order *S_ini* by *SCRs* and get *S_ini[]* =[S_{min} ,S_1...S_{max}];   //Step 1
02. Calculate *L*<S_{min} ,S_1>, intercept X_1 , V_1 ;
03. Insert X_1 to *X[]*, V_1 to *V[]*;
04. Add *L*<S_{min} ,S_1>, *X_axis*, *V_axis* to *PSS;*
05. **for** (every S_i in *S_ini*)   //Step 2
06.   ⌈ Calculate *L*<S_{min} ,S_i>, intercept X_i , V_i ;
07.   │ Insert X_i to *X[]*, V_i to *V[]*, find *S'* ;
08.   │ Stack *v_points* = Φ, Set *av_points* = Φ ;
09.   │ **do**
10.   │   ⌈ Calculate *L*<*S'*,S_i>;
11.   │   │ Find *S'.LSet* = {*L*<S_u,S_v> | S_u=*S'* or S_v=*S'*};
12.   │   │ **for** (every *L*<S_u,S_v> in *S'.LSet*)
13.   │   │   ⌈ (*x*,*v*) = intersection of *L*<*S'*,S_i> and *L*<S_u,S_v>;
14.   │   │   │ **if** ((*x*,*v*) is valid)
15.   │   │   │   ⌈ Add {*L*<S_u,S_v>,*L*<*S'*,S_i>,(*x*,*v*)} to *av_points*;
16.   │   │   │   ┤ **if** ((*x*,*v*) is not on *X* or *V* axis)
17.   │   │   │   └   Push {*L*<S_u,S_v>, (*x*,*v*)} to *v_points*;
18.   │   │ Add *L*<*S'*,S_i> to *PSS* with the endpoints ;
19.   │   └ *S'* = Get MCSS by poping *v_point*;
20.   │ **while** (*S'* !=Φ)
21.   │ **for** (every element {L_1, L_2, (*x*,*v*)} in *av_points*)   //Step 3
22.   │   ⌈ (*x'*,*v'*) = validEndpoint(L_1, L_2);
23.   │   │ Update L_1 with the endpoints (*x'*,*v'*) and (*x*,*v*);
24.   │   │ **if** (L_1 is an axis)
25.   │   └   create L_{new} in *PSS* with endpoints (x,v) and ∞ ;
26.   │ **while** (there exist intersections with less than 3 lines)
27.   └   delete the lines;
28. Return *PSS*

Function: **valid Endpoint**
Input: L_1 {(x_1,v_1), (x_2,v_2)}   // two endpoints of L_1
                   L_2 : A_2*X+ B_2*V+ C_2 =0   // equation of L_2
Output: (*x*, *v*)   //the valid endpoint of L_1

01. **if** (x_1 ==∞ | v_1 ==∞)   Return (x_2,v_2);
02. **else if** (x_2 ==∞ | v_2 ==∞)   Return (x_1,v_1);
03. $V\_L_2 = A_2$*x_1 + B_2*v_1 + C_2 ;
04. **if** (L_2 == type 1 | L_2 == type 3)
05.   **if** ($V\_L_2 < 0$)   Return (x_1,v_1);
06.   **else**   Return (x_2,v_2);
07. **else if** ($V\_L_2 < 0$)   Return (x_2,v_2);
08.   **else**   Return (x_1,v_1);

Figure 5.16 Pseudo-code of calculating PSS.

is also the third partition line to that intersection according to Lemma 5.1. This process continues until stack *v_point* is empty (line 20) which also means that we have calculated all the partition lines of S_i with its adjacent MCSSs.

- **Step 3**: update of the PSS (lines 21−27). After we add a new MCSS into the PSS, some of the old MCSSs may be overlapped. We need to update the existing partition lines in

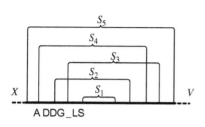
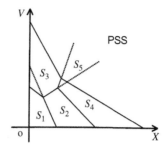

Figure 5.17 Example of a PSS.

the PSS. As all the intersections of the new joint MCSS's partition lines are saved in *av_point* in step 2, we only need to go through *av_point* and update the partition lines' endpoints (lines 21−25). To update the endpoints, first we need to find which endpoint of the partition line is overlapped by the new joint MCSS. The *valid Endpoint* function (the pseudo-code also shown in Figure 5.16) is called to find the valid endpoint that should be kept in the PSS (line 22). Then, we can update the partition line by replacing the over-lapped endpoint with the new intersection (line 23). In particular, to update the partition line on the X or V axis, we need to create a new line from the intersection to infinity because the axes cannot be overlapped (lines 24−25). After updating all the partition lines with the new intersections, we need to check all the intersections in the PSS. We delete the intersections and the corresponding partition lines that do not conform to Lemma 5.1 (lines 26−27). This is to eliminate the MCSSs that are totally overlapped by the new joint MCSS.

From the pseudo-code in Figure 5.16, we can see that the time complexity of the algorithm is $O(n_s^2 n_b)$ (lines 5−20), where n_s is the number of MCSSs in the PSS, and n_b is the number of an MCSS's adjacent MCSSs. Obviously, n_b is smaller than n_s; hence the time complexity of calculating PSS of a DDG_LS is $O(n_s^3)$.

Figure 5.17 shows an example of the PSS found by the algorithm in Figure 5.16. With the PSS, given any X and V, we can locate the corresponding MCSS with time complexity of $O(n_s)$, where classic algorithms can be found in analytic geometry [76]; hence we do not give a detailed introduction in this book. Furthermore, n_s, the number of MCSSs in the PSS is usually very small, which we will demonstrate in Chapter 7 by experimental results.

5.2.3 PSS for a General DDG (or DDG Segment)

The PSS for DDG_LS is the basis of our approach. In order to achieve the dynamic minimum cost benchmarking, we also need to calculate the PSS for general DDGs (or DDG segments). The PSS of a general DDG (or DDG segment) can be a high dimension space because the DDG may have branches where there may be more than one X and/or V value that determines the MCSS of the DDG. Although a general DDG's PSS is different from the DDG_LS's PSS, they have similar properties and can be calculated with similar algorithms. In this sub-section, for ease of understanding we first investigate the PSS of a DDG segment that only has two branches, and then extend it to a general DDG.

5.2.3.1 Three-Dimensional PSS of DDG Segment with Two Branches

Figure 5.18 shows an example of a DDG segment that has two branches. As we can see, because of two branches, the MCSS of the DDG segment is determined by three variables, which are X_1, V_2, and V_3. Hence the solution space of this DDG segment is a three-dimensional space where every MCSS occupies some space. Similar to the solution space of DDG_LS, we can find the border of two MCSSs, which is a partition plane in the three-dimensional solution space. For example, we assume that $S_{h,i,j}$ and $S_{h',i',j'}$ are two adjacent MCSSs in the solution space, where $SCR_{h,i,j} < SCR_{h',i',j'}$. The first and last stored data sets of these two strategies are in the positions shown in Figure 5.18. The equation of the partition plane is:

$$\left(\sum_{k=h'}^{h-1} v_k\right) * X_1 + \left(\sum_{k=i+1}^{i'} x_k\right) * V_2 + \left(\sum_{k=j+1}^{j'} x_k\right) * V_3 = SCR_{i',j'} - SCR_{i,j}$$

To simplify the presentation of the equation, we introduce two new notations:

$$\sum_i^j v = \begin{cases} \sum_{k=i}^{j-1} v_k, & d_i \rightarrow d_j \\ \sum_{k=j}^{i-1} v_k, & d_j \rightarrow d_i \end{cases}$$

$$\sum_i^j x = \begin{cases} \sum_{k=i+1}^{j} x_k, & d_i \rightarrow d_j \\ \sum_{k=j+1}^{i} x_k, & d_j \rightarrow d_i \end{cases}$$

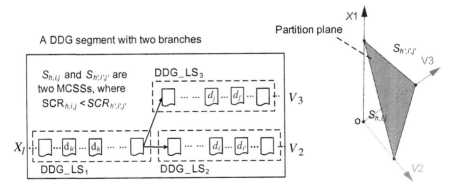

Figure 5.18 DDG segment with two branches.

Similar to the DDG_LS, the equation of the partition plane also has different forms according to the positions of the start and end data sets of the two MCSSs. In general, for the DDG segment with two branches, given two MCSSs: (1) S_p with the first stored data set d_{p1} and last stored data sets d_{p2}, d_{p3} and (2) S_q with the first stored data set d_{q1} and last stored data sets d_{q2}, d_{q3}; and $SCR_p < SCR_q$. We have the standard form of the partition plane as following:

$$Bx_1 * \left(\sum_{p_1}^{q_1} v \right) * X_1 + Bv_2 * \left(\sum_{p_2}^{q_2} x \right) * V_2 + Bv_3 * \left(\sum_{p_3}^{q_3} x \right) * V_3 = SCR_q - SCR_p$$

$$Bx_1 \begin{cases} -1, & d_{p_1} \to d_{q_1} \\ 0, & d_{p_1} = d_{q_1} \\ 1, & d_{q_1} \to d_{p_1} \end{cases} \quad Bv_2 \begin{cases} -1 & d_{q_2} \to d_{p_2} \\ 0 & d_{p_2} = d_{q_2} \\ 1 & d_{p_2} \to d_{q_2} \end{cases} \quad Bv_3 \begin{cases} -1 & d_{q_3} \to d_{p_3} \\ 0 & d_{p_3} = d_{q_3} \\ 1 & d_{p_3} \to d_{q_3} \end{cases}$$

Similar to the DDG_LS, the DDG segment with two branches also has a PSS, in which the partition planes of the MCSSs intersect with each other and partition the solution space into different spaces. For any given values of X_1, V_2, V_3, we can locate an MCSS in the PSS for storing the DDG segment, if we know the distribution of MCSSs in the PSS. The three-dimensional PSS has similar properties to the PSS of DDG_LS. In order to calculate the PSS, we introduce another two lemmas, which describe important properties of the intersection lines and points in the three-dimensional PSS.

Lemma 5.2 *In a three-dimensional PSS, for three MCSSs, if any two of them are adjacent to each other, then the three partition planes intersect in one line.*

Figure 5.19 shows an example of Lemma 5.2. In Figure 5.19A, S_a, S_b, S_c are three MCSSs of a DDG segment with two branches. We assume that $SCR_a < SCR_b < SCR_c$ and the start and end data sets of the three MCSSs have the following relationships: $d_{c_1} \to d_{b_1} \to d_{a_1}$, $d_{a_2} \to d_{b_2} \to d_{c_2}$, $d_{a_3} \to d_{b_3} \to d_{c_3}$. Then we have three partition planes of S_a, S_b, S_c as follows:

$$P < S_a, S_b > : \left(\sum_{a_1}^{b_1} v \right) * X_1 + \left(\sum_{a_2}^{b_2} x \right) * V_2 + \left(\sum_{a_3}^{b_3} x \right) * V_3 = SCR_b - SCR_a$$

$$P < S_b, S_c > : \left(\sum_{b_1}^{c_1} v \right) * X_1 + \left(\sum_{b_2}^{c_2} x \right) * V_2 + \left(\sum_{b_3}^{c_3} x \right) * V_3 = SCR_c - SCR_b$$

$$P < S_a, S_c > : \left(\sum_{a_1}^{c_1} v \right) * X_1 + \left(\sum_{a_2}^{c_2} x \right) * V_2 + \left(\sum_{a_3}^{c_3} x \right) * V_3 = SCR_c - SCR_a$$

As shown in Figure 5.19B, $P < S_a, S_b >$ is the partition plane of S_a and S_b, $P < S_b, S_c >$ is the partition plane of S_b and S_c, and $P < S_a, S_c >$ is the partition

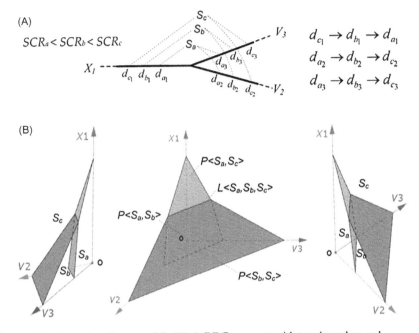

Figure 5.19 Example of Lemma 5.2. (A) A DDG segment with two branches and (B) a three-dimensional PSS viewed from different angles.

plane of S_a and S_c. According to Lemma 5.2, the three partition planes intersect in one line $L < S_a, S_b, S_c >$.

Lemma 5.3 *In a three-dimensional PSS, for four MCSSs, if any three of them intersect in a different line, then the four intersection lines intersect at one point.*

Figure 5.20 shows an example of Lemma 5.3. In Figure 5.20, S_a, S_b, S_c and S_e are four MCSSs in the PSS and the partition planes denote the borders of the occupied spaces by the MCSSs. We assume that L_{AB} (the line passing point A and point B in Figure 5.20) is the intersection line of S_a, S_b and S_c; L_{AC} is the intersection line of S_a, S_c and S_e; L_{AD} is the intersection line of S_a, S_b and S_e and L_{AE} is the intersection line of S_b, S_c and S_e. According to Lemma 5.3, the four intersection lines intersect at point A.

5.2.3.2 High-Dimensional PSS of a General DDG

After the two- and three-dimensional illustration and description to assist in understanding, we now discuss the general case. In a general DDG segment, there may exist multiple branches; hence there are more variables (i.e. more X and V dimensions) that impact the MCSS of the DDG segment. This makes the general DDG segment's PSS a high-dimensional space, where the number of the dimensions is the total number of different X and V variables. In an n dimension PSS, every

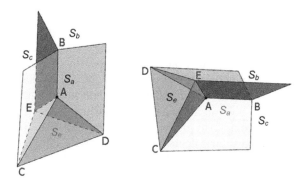

Figure 5.20 Example of Lemma 5.3 − four MCSSs' intersection in a three-dimensional PSS, viewed from different angles.

MCSS occupies some n dimension space, where we can calculate the border of every two MCSSs in the similar way as the three-dimensional PSS.

For an n dimension PSS, we assume that there be m branches with preceding data sets (i.e. different X dimensions), hence $n-m$ branches with succeeding data sets (i.e. different V dimensions). Given two MCSSs (1) S_p with the first stored data sets $d_{p\_1}, d_{p\_2}, \ldots, d_{p\_m}$ in the m different X dimension branches and the last stored data sets $d_{p\_(m+1)}, d_{p\_(m+2)}, \ldots, d_{p\_n}$ in the $n-m$ different V dimension branches and (2) S_q with the first stored data sets $d_{q\_1}, d_{q\_2}, \ldots, d_{q\_m}$ in the m different X dimension branches and the last stored data sets $d_{q\_(m+1)}, d_{q\_(m+2)}, \ldots, d_{q\_n}$ in the $n-m$ different V dimension branches, and $SCR_p < SCR_q$, then the border of S_p and S_q in the n dimension space is: {set as display equation}

$$\sum_{i=1}^{m}\left(Bx_i * \left(\sum_{p_i}^{q_i} v\right) * X_i\right) + \sum_{j=m+1}^{n}\left(Bv_j * \left(\sum_{p_j}^{q_j} x\right) * V_j\right) = SCR_q - SCR_p$$

$$Bx_i = \begin{cases} -1, & d_{p_i} \to d_{q_i} \\ 0, & d_{p_i} = d_{q_i} \\ 1, & d_{q_i} \to d_{p_i} \end{cases} \qquad Bv_j = \begin{cases} -1 & d_{q_j} \to d_{p_j} \\ 0 & d_{p_j} = d_{q_j} \\ 1 & d_{p_j} \to d_{q_j} \end{cases}$$

From the equation above, we can see that the border of two MCSSs in an n dimensions PSS is an n-variable linear equation, which is an $(n-1)$ dimension space itself. In order to calculate the PSS of a general DDG segment, we need to investigate the intersections of the MCSSs in the n dimension space. We generalise Lemmas 5.1−5.3 to the n dimension PSS of a general DDG segment and propose Theorem 5.6 as follows.

Theorem 5.6 *In an n dimension PSS, for i MCSSs where* $i \in \{2, 3, \ldots, (n+1)\}$, *if any* $(i-1)$ *of the i MCSSs intersects in a different* $(n-i+2)$ *dimension space, then the i MCSSs intersect in an* $(n-i+1)$ *dimension space.*

Based on Theorem 5.6, given the initial MCSS set of a general DDG segment (i.e. *S_ini*), we can design an algorithm to calculate the PSS in a similar way to the algorithm for calculating the PSS for DDG_LS. In Section 5.2.4, we will introduce how to derive *S_ini* of a general DDG segment without calling the CTT-SP algorithm on it. For a PSS with n_d dimensions, the border of MCSSs are n_d-variable linear equations and we need to solve the n_d-variable linear equations system to calculate an intersection point in the solution space which has a time complexity of $O(n_d^3)$. Hence the time complexity of calculating a general DDG segment's PSS is n_d^3 times of the complexity for calculating the DDG_LS's PSS, which is $O(n_s^3 n_d^3)$. Similarly, locating the MCSS in the high-dimensional PSS with given X and V values is also n_d^3 times complex than locating an MCSS in the two-dimensional PSS, which is $O(n_s n_d^3)$.

5.2.4 Dynamic On-the-Fly Minimum Cost Benchmarking

The purpose of calculating the PSS for DDG segment is for dynamic minimum cost benchmarking. The philosophy of our approach is that we merge the PSSs of the DDG_LSs to derive the PSS of the whole DDG and save all the calculated PSSs along this process. Taking advantage of the pre-calculated results (i.e. the saved PSSs), whenever the application cost changes, we only need to recalculate the local DDG_LS's PSS and quickly derive the new minimum cost benchmark for the whole DDG. By dynamically keeping the minimum cost benchmark updated, benchmarking requests can be instantly responded to on the fly.

5.2.4.1 Minimum Cost Benchmarking by Merging and Saving PSSs in a Hierarchy

To calculate the minimum cost benchmark with our approach, we need to merge the DDG segments' PSSs in order to get the PSS of the whole DDG, from which we can locate the MCSS. To merge the PSSs of two DDG segments, we need to introduce another theorem.

Theorem 5.7 *Given* DDG *segment* $\{d_1, d_2, \ldots, d_m\}$ *with* PSS_1, DDG *segment* $\{d_{m+1}, d_{m+2}, \ldots, d_n\}$ *with* PSS_2, *and the merged* DDG *segment* $\{d_1, d_2, \ldots, d_m, d_{m+1}, d_{m+2}, \ldots, d_n\}$ *with* PSS. *Then we have:*

$$\forall S \in PSS \Rightarrow \begin{cases} S = S_1 \cup S_2, \quad S_1 \in PSS_1 \quad S_2 \in PSS_2 \\ SCR = SCR_1 + \left(\sum_{k=j+1}^{m} x_k \right) * \left(\sum_{k=m+1}^{i-1} v_k \right) + SCR_2 \end{cases}$$

where d_j is the last stored data set in the first DDG *segment and d_i is the first stored data set in the second* DDG *segment.*

Theorem 5.7 tells us that (i) the MCSSs in a larger DDG segment's PSS (i.e. S) are combined by the MCSSs in its sub-DDG segments' PSSs (i.e. S_1, S_2), which means that we can calculate the PSS of the larger DDG segment by merging the PSSs of its sub-DDG segments and do not need to call the CTT-SP algorithm on the larger DDG segment and (ii) the cost rate of the MCSS in the larger DDG segment (i.e. SCR) is the sum of cost rates of its sub-DDG segments' MCSSs (i.e. SCR_1, SCR_2) and a parameter which is $(\sum_{k=j+1}^{m} x_k) * (\sum_{k=m+1}^{i-1} v_k)$. This parameter indicates the cost rate compensation for the data sets in the connecting branches of the two sub-DDG segments, i.e. the generation cost rate of data sets in DDG segment $\{d_{j+1}, d_{j+2}, \ldots, d_m\}$ for regenerating data sets in the DDG segment $\{d_{m+1}, d_{m+2}, \ldots, d_{i-1}\}$. Figure 5.21 further shows an example of Theorem 5.7 to merge two linear DDG segments.

Figure 5.22 shows the pseudo-code of merging two PSSs. In this algorithm, we first find the MCSS candidate set for the merged PSS (i.e. S_All) by combining the

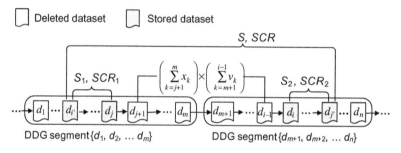

Figure 5.21 Example of merging two linear DDG segments.

Algorithm: **Merge PSSs**
Input: PSS_1 of DDG segment $\{d_1, d_2, \ldots d_m\}$
PSS_2 of DDG segment $\{d_{m+1}, d_{m+2}, \ldots d_n\}$
Output: PSS for the merged DDG segment

01. $S\_All = \Phi$, $SCR_{max} = \infty$;
02. **for** (every MCSS S' in PSS_1)
03.   **for** (every MCSS S'' in PSS_2)
04.   Add $S = S' \cup S''$ to S_All;
05. $SCR = SCR' + \left(\sum_{k=j+1}^{m} x_k \right) * \left(\sum_{k=m+1}^{i-1} v_k \right) + SCR''$;
06.   **if** (the first and last datasets in all the branches are all stored in S and $SCR < SCR_{max}$)
07. $SCR_{max} = SCR$;
08. **for** (every MCSS S in S_All)
09.   **if** ($SCR > SCR_{max}$)
10.   Delete S from S_All ;
11. S_ini = Eliminate S_All (S_All); $//O(n_s^2)$
12. PSS = Calculate PSS (S_ini); $//O(n_s^3 n_d^3)$
13. Return PSS;

Figure 5.22 Pseudo-code for merging PSSs.

MCSSs in the two sub-PSSs (lines $1-7$). During this process we also calculate the SCR for every MCSS (line 5) and find the upper bound for SCR_{max} (lines $6-7$). Next, we eliminate the invalid MCSSs from S_All, which includes two sub-steps: deleting the MCSSs with invalid SCR values (lines $8-10$) and calling the elimination algorithm (see Figure 5.14) to derive S_ini (line 11). Then we call the PSS calculation algorithm (see Figure 5.16) to calculate the PSS of the merged DDG segment (line 12). From the pseudo-code, we can clearly see that the time complexity of merging two PSSs is the same as that of the calculation of the PSS, which is $O(n_s^3 n_d^3)$.

To calculate the PSS of a general DDG in the cloud, we can calculate all the PSSs of its sub-DDG_LSs and gradually merge them to derive the PSS of the whole DDG. In order to achieve dynamic benchmarking, we need to save not only the PSSs of the DDG_LSs but also the PSSs calculated during the merging process. In our approach, we use a hierarchy data structure to save all the PSSs of a DDG, where an example of saving the PSS of a DDG with three sub-DDG_LSs is shown in Figure 5.23.

In the PSS hierarchy, the level indicates the number of DDG_LSs merged in the PSS of the DDG segments at that level. For example, in Figure 5.23, the DDG_LSs' PSSs are saved at *Level* 1 of the hierarchy. *Level* 2 saves the PSSs of the DDG segments, which are connected by two DDG_LSs, e.g. PSS_{12} is the PSS of DDG segment combined by DDG_LS_1 and DDG_LS_2. *Level* 3 saves the PSS of the whole DDG, where we can see that the number of the hierarchy levels equals the number of DDG_LSs in the whole DDG. Furthermore, there are links between the levels in the hierarchy. A link between two PSSs at *Levels* i and $i + 1$ in the hierarchy means the corresponding DDG segment of the PSS at *Level* $i + 1$ contains the DDG segment of the PSS at *Level* i, e.g. in Figure 5.23, there is a link between PSS_1 and PSS_{12} because the DDG segment combined by DDG_LS_1 and DDG_LS_2 contains DDG_LS_1.

In the hierarchy, the highest level (e.g. Level 3 in Figure 5.23) saves the PSS of the whole DDG. From this PSS we can derive the MCSS and the corresponding SCR of the whole DDG, which is the minimum cost benchmark (i.e. SCR) that we can either proactively report or instantly respond to benchmarking requests. Next, we will introduce how to dynamically keep this benchmark updated.

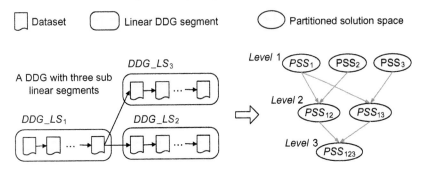

Figure 5.23 Saving all the PSSs of a DDG in a hierarchy.

5.2.4.2   Updating of the Minimum Cost Benchmark on the Fly

Cloud is a dynamic environment. As time goes on, new data sets are generated in the cloud and the existing data sets' usage frequencies may also change. Hence the minimum cost benchmark of storing the data sets would also change accordingly. By taking the advantage of the PSS hierarchy, we can dynamically calculate the new minimum cost benchmark on the fly. There are two situations that we need to deal with:

1. New data sets are generated in the cloud.

   The algorithm pseudo-code of calculating the new minimum cost benchmark of this situation is shown in Figure 5.24. Assuming that the new data sets be in a DDG_LS (if not, we take its sub-DDG_LS), first we add it to the whole DDG and calculate its PSS, denoted as *PSS_new* (lines 1−3). Next, for every MCSS in *PSS_new*, we locate the corresponding MCSS from the original DDG's PSS (lines 5−7) and calculate the cost rate of the whole DDG, i.e. SCR (line 8). Then, we find the minimum SCR as the new minimum cost benchmark for the whole DDG and the corresponding storage strategy as the new MCSS (lines 9−11). In this whole process, we need to calculate only the PSS of the new DDG_LS, which is usually small in size, and the PSS of the original DDG has already been pre-calculated and saved in the hierarchy. Hence we can quickly update the minimum cost benchmark. For example, in Figure 5.25A, for the new DDG_LS_4, we calculate PSS_4 and connect it with the existing PSS_{123} in the hierarchy to derive the updated minimum cost benchmark and the MCSS of the whole DDG.

   After calculating the new minimum cost benchmark, we have to update the PSS hierarchy for the new DDG_LS. For every newly added PSS at *Level i* of the hierarchy (starting from *Level* 1 to the highest level), we find its connected DDG_LS in the whole DDG

Algorithm:	**Generate new datasets**	
Input:	*DDG_LS*	//New datasets
	PSS	//PSS of the whole DDG
Output:	S	//MCSS of the whole DDG
	SCR	//Updated minimum cost benchmark

01. $S_All = $ Find $S\_All\ (DDG\_LS)$;
02. $S_ini = $ Eliminate S_All (S_All); $//O(n_s{}^2)$
03. $PSS_new = $ Calculate PSS (S_ini); $//O(n_s{}^3 n_d{}^3)$
04. $SCR = \infty$; $S = \Phi$;
05. **for** (every $S_{i,j}$ in PSS_new)
06. $\quad V = \sum_{k=1}^{i-1} v_k$;
07. $\quad S_{temp} = PSS.$Locate $(0,...0,V)$;
08. $\quad SCR_{min} = SCR_{temp} + \left(\sum_{k=j'+1}^{n} x_k \right) * V + SCR_{i,j}$;
09. $\quad$ **if** $(SCR > SCR_{min})$
10. $\quad\quad S = S_{temp} \cup S_{i,j}$;
11. $\quad\quad SCR = SCR_{min}$;
12. Return S, SCR;

Figure 5.24 Pseudo-code for calculating new minimum cost benchmark when new data sets are generated.

(A)   (B)

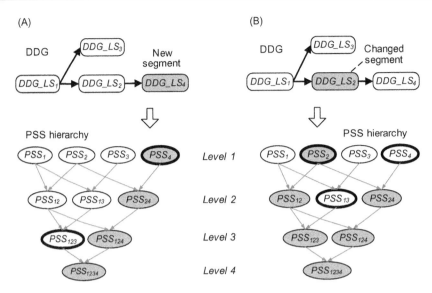

Figure 5.25 Updating the PSS hierarchy when the DDG is changed. Updating the PSS hierarchy (A) for adding a new segment to DDG and (B) for changing the PSS of a segment in the DDG.

and connect them to form a new segment. We calculate the PSS of the new segment and add it to *Level* $i + 1$ of the hierarchy as well as the corresponding links between the two levels. An example of updating the PSS hierarchy in this situation is shown in Figure 5.25A, where the shadowed PSSs are the new ones that we add to the hierarchy after adding PSS_4.

2. Existing data sets' usage frequencies are changed.

In this situation, we first find the DDG_LS that contains the data sets whose usage frequencies are changed. As shown in the pseudo-code in Figure 5.26, we also need to calculate the DDG_LS's PSS at the beginning (lines 1−3). Then, we find the PSSs of the remaining parts of the whole DDG, except for the changed DDG_LS, and save them in a set, i.e. *PSS_Set* (line 4). Next, for every MCSS in the new PSS (line 6), we calculate the X and V values (line 7) to locate the corresponding MCSSs of the DDG segments that are connected to the changed DDG_LS from PSSs in *PSS_Set* (lines 8−17). We also calculate the corresponding cost rate of the whole DDG, i.e. SCR (line 18). Then, we find the minimum SCR as the updated minimum cost benchmark for the whole DDG and the corresponding storage strategy as the new MCSS (lines 19−20). In this whole process, when calculating the PSS of the changed DDG_LS, we only update the weights of some edges in the existing CTT and do not need to create a new one. Furthermore, the PSSs of DDG segments in *PSS_Set* have already been pre-calculated and saved in the hierarchy. Hence we can quickly update the minimum cost benchmark. For example, in Figure 5.25B, we recalculate PSS_2 for changed DDG_LS_2. To derive the updated minimum cost benchmark for the whole DDG, we connect new PSS_2 with PSS_{13} and PSS_4 in *PSS_Set*, which are the remaining parts of the whole DDG except DDG_LS_2.

Algorithm:	Change usage frequency	
Input:	DDG_LS_i	//With the changed dataset
	The PSS hierarchy	
Output:	S	//MCSS of the whole DDG
	SCR	//Updated minimum cost benchmark

01. S_All = Find S_All (DDG_LS_i);
02. S_ini = Eliminate S_All (S_All); $//O(n_s^2)$
03. PSS_new = Calculate PSS (S_ini); $//O(n_s^3 n_d^3)$
04. PSS_Set = PSSs of the DDG segments connecting to DDG_LS_i;
05. $SCR = \infty$; $S = S' = \Phi$;
06. for (every $S_{i,j}$ in PSS_new)
07. $\quad\left[\quad V = \sum_{k=1}^{i-1} v_k; \quad X = \sum_{k=j+1}^{m} x_k ;\right.$
08. $\quad\quad$ for (every PSS_h in PSS_Set)
09. $\quad\quad\quad$ if (PSS_h is preceding to PSS_new)
10. $\quad\quad\quad\quad S_{temp} = PSS_h$.Locate $(0,...0,V)$;
11. $\quad\quad\quad\quad SCR_{min} = SCR_{temp} + \left(\sum_{k=j'+1}^{n} x_k\right) * V$;
12. $\quad\quad\quad$ eles if (PSS_h is succeeding to PSS_new)
13. $\quad\quad\quad\quad S_{temp} = PSS_h$.Locate $(0,...0,X)$;
14. $\quad\quad\quad\quad SCR_{min} = SCR_{temp} + \left(\sum_{k=1}^{i'-1} v_k\right) * X$;
15. $\quad\quad\quad$ else $\quad S_{temp} = PSS_h$.Locate $(0,...0,X,V)$;
16. $\quad\quad\quad\quad SCR_{min} = SCR_{temp} + \left(\sum_{k=1}^{i'-1} v_k\right) * X + \left(\sum_{k=j'+1}^{n} x_k\right) * V$;
17. $\quad\quad\quad S' = S' \cup S_{temp}$;
18. $\quad\quad SCR_{min} += SCR_{i,j}$;
19. $\quad\quad$ if ($SCR > SCR_{min}$) $\quad S = S' \cup S_{i,j}$;
20. $\quad\quad\quad\quad\quad\quad\quad\quad SCR = SCR_{min}$;
21. Return S, SCR;

Figure 5.26 Pseudo-code for calculating new minimum cost benchmark when data sets' usage frequencies are changed.

After calculating the new minimum cost benchmark, we also need to update the PSS hierarchy for the changed PSS. For every changed PSS at *Level i* of the hierarchy (starting from *Level* 1 to the highest level), we find the PSSs at *Level i* + 1 that are linked with it and update them all. An example of updating the PSS hierarchy in this situation is shown in Figure 5.25B, where the shadowed PSSs are the new ones that we need to update in the hierarchy after changing PSS_2.

In terms of efficiency, our approach can instantly respond to users' benchmarking requests by keeping the minimum cost benchmark updated on the fly. Whenever new data sets are generated and/or existing data sets' usage frequencies are changed, our algorithm can quickly calculate the updated minimum cost benchmark in $O(n_s^3 n_d^3)$ (see Figures 5.24 and 5.26), where all the parameters are for the local DDG_LS, which are usually very small. The total time complexity of our benchmarking approach includes updating the hierarchy, which is used to save the PSSs. We use m to denote the number of DDG_LS in the whole DDG. In the situation of new data sets generation, we need to add one new PSS to every level of the PSS hierarchy (see Figure 5.25A), where the number of the levels equals the number of DDG_LSs in the whole DDG; hence the time complexity is $O(mn_s^3 n_d^3)$. In the case of existing data sets' usage frequencies changing, we have to recalculate more than one PSS (i.e. in the magnitude of m) in every level of the hierarchy (see Figure 5.25B); hence the time complexity is $O(m^2 n_s^3 n_d^3)$.

In Chapter 7, we will use experimental results to further demonstrate this dynamic on-the-fly benchmarking approach.

5.3 Summary

In this chapter, we propose two minimum cost benchmarking approaches for scientific applications in the cloud. Benchmarking is the process of calculating the minimum cost rate of storing the application data sets in the cloud, which achieves the best trade-off between computation and storage. This benchmark can be utilised to evaluate the cost-effectiveness of all data sets storage strategies. Our two novel benchmarking approaches are summarised as follows.

The static on-demand benchmarking approach is suitable for situations in which only occasional benchmarking is requested. In this situation the benchmarking is a one-time-only computation provided as an on-demand service. In this approach, the novel CTT-SP algorithm is designed, which solves a seemingly NP-hard problem in a polynomial time complexity.

The dynamic on-the-fly benchmarking approach is suitable for situations in which more frequent benchmarking is requested at run time. In these situations, the benchmarking service is delivered on the fly to instantly respond to benchmarking requests. In this approach, we thoroughly investigated the issue of computation and storage trade-off and proposed a novel concept of PSS to save the pre-calculated MCSSs. By utilising the pre-calculated results, whenever the application cost changes in the cloud, we can quickly calculate the new minimum cost benchmark. By dynamically keeping the benchmark updated, benchmarking requests can be instantly responded to on the fly.

6 Cost-Effective Data Set Storage Strategies

Due to the pay-as-you-go model, we design cost-effective data set storage strategies for users based on the trade-off between computation and storage in the cloud. Different from benchmarking, in practice, the MCSS may not be the ultimate goal for the applications because storage strategies should be efficient for users to facilitate at run-time in the cloud and may need to take users' tolerance of data-accessing delay into consideration. This chapter is organised as follows.

In Section 6.1, by investigating users' tolerance of data-accessing delay and users' preferences regarding the storage of particular data sets, we introduce two new attributes of the data sets in DDG accordingly [89]. With the new attributes and corresponding mechanisms, the storage strategies can (a) guarantee that all the application data sets' regenerations fulfil users' tolerance of data-accessing delays and (b) allow users to store some data sets with a higher cost according to their preferences.

In Section 6.2, we design an innovative cost-rate-based storage strategy. In this strategy, we directly compare the generation cost rate and storage cost rate for every data set to decide its storage status. The strategy can guarantee that the stored data sets in the system are all necessary, and can dynamically check whether the regenerated data sets need to be stored and, if so, adjust the storage strategy accordingly. This strategy is highly efficient with fairly reasonable cost-effectiveness. This section is mainly based on our work presented in [87,91].

In Section 6.3, we design an innovative local-optimisation-based storage strategy. In this strategy, we divide the DDG with large number of application data sets into small linear segments (DDG_LS). By partially utilising an enhanced linear CTT-SP algorithm, we can find the MCSS for the DDG_LS satisfying users' requirements. Hence we achieve the localised optimisation in the storage strategy. This strategy is highly cost effective with very reasonable run-time efficiency. This section is mainly based on our work presented in [89].

6.1 Data-Accessing Delay and Users' Preferences in Storage Strategies

With the excessive computation and storage resources in the cloud, users can flexibly choose storage strategies for application-generated data sets. The CTT-SP algorithm proposed in Section 5.1 can find the MCSS for a DDG. If a generated application data set has been deleted to save the storage cost, we have to regenerate it whenever it needs to be reused. Regeneration not only requires computation resources but also causes a delay in accessing the data, i.e. waiting for the data set to be ready. Depending on the requirements of applications, users may have different tolerance of computation delays for accessing different data sets. Some data sets are stored at a higher cost due to users' preferences, such as the need for immediate data access. Furthermore, knowing the minimum cost benchmark, users may wish to spend more money on storing more data sets in order to reduce the average computation delay.

In this subsection, we enhance the linear CTT-SP algorithm by introducing two new parameters which can represent users' preferences and provide users with some flexibility in using the storage strategy. The two parameters are denoted as T and λ.

- T is the parameter used to represent users' tolerance of data-accessing delays. Users need to inform the cloud service provider about which data sets they have requirements of availabilities. For a data set d_i which needs regeneration, T_i is the delay time that users can tolerate when they want to access it. Furthermore, T is also related to the requirements of applications. For example, some applications may have fixed time constraints [59], such as the weather forecast application. In this situation, for some particular data sets, the value for T_i can be set according to the starting time and finishing time (i.e. deadline) of the application. In other words, T is the time constraint of data sets' regeneration. In the storage strategy, the regeneration time of any deleted data set d_i cannot exceed its T_i. In particular, if T_i is smaller than the generation time of data set d_i itself (i.e. $T_i < x_i/Price_{cpu}$, where $Price_{cpu}$ is the price of computation resources used to regenerate d_i in the cloud), then we have to store d_i, no matter how expensive d_i's storage cost is.

- λ is the parameter used to adjust the storage strategy when users have extra budget on top of the minimum cost benchmark to store more data sets in order to reduce the average data sets' accessing time. Based on users' extra budget, we can calculate a proper value of λ, which is between 0 and 1.[1] We multiply every data set d_i's storage cost rate (i.e. y_i) by λ, and use it to compare with d_i's regeneration cost rate (i.e. $genCost(d_i)^*v_i$) to decide its storage status. Hence, more data sets tend to be stored and, literally speaking, they will be deleted only when their storage cost rates are $(1/\lambda)$ times higher than their regeneration cost rates. For example, $\lambda_i = 0.8$ means that users are willing to store data sets with a storage cost up to 1.25 times higher than the regeneration cost.

These two attributes are generic for the data set storage strategies. With these two attributes, we design two new run-time storage strategies for different situations in the cloud.

6.2   Cost-Rate-Based Storage Strategy

In this storage strategy, for every data set in the cloud, we directly compare the generation cost rate and storage cost rate of the data set itself to decide its storage

---

[1] Please refer to Appendix C for the details of how to calculate the value of λ based on users' budget.

status. This strategy is highly efficient. The details of algorithms and cost-effectiveness analysis are described next in this section.

6.2.1   Algorithms for the Strategy

We design three algorithms to handle all three situations in the cloud to decide the proper storage status of the application data sets. We analyse the time complexity of the algorithms in this subsection and further evaluate the efficiency of this cost-rate-based strategy by experiments described in Section 7.3.2.

6.2.1.1   Algorithm for Deciding Newly Generated Data Sets' Storage Status

We assume d_i is a newly generated data set. The pseudo-code of this algorithm is shown in Figure 6.1.

First, we add its information to the DDG (line 1). We add edges pointing to d_i from its provenance data sets and initialise its attributes. As d_i is new and obviously does not have a usage history yet, we use the average value in the system as the initial value for d_i's usage frequency.

Next, we check whether d_i should be stored or not (lines 2–10). First, we check whether the generation time of d_i can satisfy users' tolerance of data-accessing delay (line 2). If not, we store d_i (line 3). Then we only compare the generation cost rate of d_i with its storage cost rate multiplied by λ_i, which are $genCost(d_i)^*v_i$ and $y_i^*\lambda_i$ (line 5). If the generation cost rate is larger than the storage cost rate, we store d_i (line 6); otherwise, we delete d_i (line 8).

From the pseudo-code in Figure 6.1, we can see that the worst-case time complexity of the algorithm is $O(n_a)$ (i.e., calculating $genCost(d_i)$ in line 2), where n_a is the largest number of a data set's deleted predecessors in the DDG.

Algorithm:	**Decide storage status of a newly generated dataset**
Input:	Newly generated dataset d_i ;
	DDG ;
Output:	f_i ; //Storage status of d_i

01. **add** d_i's information to DDG ;
02. **if** ($genCost(d_i)\big/Price_{cpu} > T_i$)
03. f_i = "stored" ;   //decide to store d_i
04. **else**
05.   ⎡ **if** ($genCost(d_i)*v_i > y_i*\lambda_i$)
06.   ⎥ f_i = "stored" ;   //decide to store d_i
07.   ⎥ **else**
08.   ⎣ f_i = "$deleted$" ;   //decide to delete d_i
09. Return f_i ;   //storage status of d_i

Figure 6.1 Algorithm for deciding newly generated data sets' storage status.

Algorithm:	Decide storage status of a stored dataset
Input:	Stored dataset d_i ;
	DDG ;
Output:	f_i ; //Storage status of d_i

01. **if** ($genCost(d_i)/Price_{cpu} > T_i$)
02.   Return f_i = "stored" ;
03. **else**
04.   **for** (every deleted successor d_k of d_i)
05.   **if** (($genCost(d_i) + genCost(d_k))/Price_{cpu} > T_k$)
06.   Return f_i = "stored" ;
07. $v \mathrel{+}= v_k$;
08.   **if** ($genCost(d_i) * v > y_i * \lambda_i$)
09.   Return f_i = "stored" ;
10.   **else**
11.   Return f_i = "deleted" ;

Figure 6.2 Algorithm for deciding stored data sets' storage status.

6.2.1.2 Algorithm for Deciding Stored Data Sets' Storage Status Due to Usage Frequencies Change

We assume d_i is a stored data set whose usage frequency is changed in the cloud. We need to recalculate its storage status. The pseudo-code of this algorithm is shown in Figure 6.2.

First, we check whether the generation time of d_i can satisfy users' tolerance of data-accessing delays (line 1). If not, we keep it stored (line 2). Because d_i is stored originally, the deletion will increase the generation cost and time of its deleted successors. Hence we need to further check whether the generation time of d_i's deleted successors can satisfy users' tolerance of data-accessing delay (lines 4−7). If not, we keep d_i stored (line 6). Then we compare d_i's generation cost rate with its storage cost rate in order to decide its storage status (lines 8−11).

From the pseudo-code in Figure 6.2, we can see that the worst-case time complexity of the algorithm is $O(n_a n_b)$ (lines 4 and 5), where n_a is discussed in Section 6.2.1.1 and n_b here is the largest number of a data set's deleted successors in the DDG.

6.2.1.3 Algorithm for Deciding Regenerated Data Sets' Storage Status

We assume that d_i is a deleted data set in the cloud. When we regenerate it for reuse, we have to recalculate its storage status after the reuse. The pseudo-code of this algorithm is shown in Figure 6.3.

Because d_i is originally a deleted data set, the storage of d_i reduces the generation cost of its deleted successors. We need to take this cost reduction into consideration when calculating d_i's generation cost rate (lines 1−2). Next, we compare d_i's generation cost rate with its storage cost rate in order to decide its storage status (lines 3−8). Notably, if d_i is stored, it will not need its stored predecessors (i.e., $provSet_i$) for regeneration, and its stored successors' generation costs are also

---

Algorithm: **Decide storage status of a regenerated dataset**
Input: Regenerated dataset d_i ;
                 DDG ;
Output: f_i ;   //Storage status of d_i

---

01. **for** (every deleted successor d_k of d_i)
02. $v += v_k$;
03. **if** ($genCost(d_i)*(v_i + v) > y_i * \lambda_i$)
04. $\lceil$ $f_i =$ "stored" ;
05. $\{$ **for** (every stored predecessor and successor d_j of d_i)
06. $\lfloor$ recalculate the storage status of d_j ;
07. **else**
08. $f_i =$ "deleted" ;
09. Return f_i ;

Figure 6.3 Algorithm for deciding regenerated data sets' storage status.

reduced; hence these stored predecessors and successors may not need to be stored anymore. We need to recalculate their storage statuses (lines 5−6).

From the pseudo-code in Figure 6.3, we can see that the worst-case time complexity of the algorithm is $O(n_a n_b n_c)$ (lines 5 and 6), where n_a and n_b are discussed in Sections 6.2.1.1 and 6.2.1.2, respectively, and n_c here is the largest number of a data set's stored predecessors and successors in the DDG. The efficiency of running the strategy will be evaluated in Section 7.3.2.

6.2.2 Cost-Effectiveness Analysis

To analyse the cost-effectiveness of this cost-rate-based storage strategy, we need to introduce the following lemma and theorem.

Lemma 6.1 *The deletion of a stored data set in the DDG does not affect the storage status of other stored data sets.*

Theorem 6.1 *If a deleted data set is stored, only its adjacent stored predecessors and successors in the DDG may need to be deleted to reduce the application cost.*

Lemma 6.1 and Theorem 6.1 guarantee that the data sets stored by the algorithms in our cost-rate-based storage strategy are all necessary, which means that the deletion of any data set will bring cost increase of the application in the cloud. The cost-effectiveness of this strategy will be further evaluated by experiments in Section 7.3.1.

6.3   Local-Optimisation-Based Storage Strategy

In this storage strategy, we utilise the linear CTT-SP algorithm presented in Section 5.1.1 and enhance it by incorporating the two new attributes $\langle T_i, \lambda_i \rangle$ addressed in Section 6.1, so that it can find the MCSS for linear DDG segments by satisfying users' tolerance of computation delay and preference on storage. We use the enhanced CTT-SP algorithm on the linear segments in the large DDG, which achieves a localised optimisation. The details of algorithms and cost-effectiveness analysis are described next in this section.

6.3.1 Algorithms and Rules for the Strategy

First, we introduce the enhanced CTT-SP algorithm. Then, we describe the local-optimisation-based storage strategy with the rules for using the enhanced CTT-SP algorithms in different situations.

6.3.1.1 Enhanced CTT-SP Algorithm for Linear DDG

The linear CTT-SP algorithm is described in Section 5.1.1. In the algorithm, we have:

$$(\forall\, d_i, d_j \in \text{DDG} \wedge d_i \rightarrow d_j) \Rightarrow \exists e\langle d_i, d_j\rangle$$

and the weight of the edge, i.e., $\omega\langle d_i, d_j\rangle$, means 'the sum of cost rates of d_j and the data sets between d_i and d_j, supposing that only d_i and d_j be stored and rest of the data sets between d_i and d_j all be deleted'.

To incorporate the delay tolerance attribute T, in the enhanced linear CTT-SP algorithm, the edge $e\langle d_i, d_j\rangle$ has to further satisfy the condition:

$$e\langle d_i, d_j\rangle \Rightarrow \forall\, d_k \in \text{DDG} \wedge (d_i \rightarrow d_k \rightarrow d_j) \wedge \left(\frac{genCost(d_k)}{Price_{cpu}} < T_k \right)$$

With this condition, long cost edges may be eliminated from the CTT. This guarantees that in all the storage strategies of the DDG found by the algorithm, the regeneration time for every deleted data set d_i, is smaller than T_i.

To incorporate the users' preference attribute λ, in the enhanced linear CTT-SP algorithm, we set the weight of a cost edge in CTT as

$$\omega\langle d_i, d_j\rangle = y_j * \lambda_j + \sum_{\{d_k | d_k \in \text{DDG} \wedge d_i \rightarrow d_k \rightarrow d_j\}} (genCost(d_k) * v_k)$$

In Figure 6.4, we demonstrate a simple example of constructing the CTT for a DDG that only has three data sets, using the enhanced linear CTT-SP algorithm and supposing that all the edges satisfy the computation delay tolerance.

Based on the discussion above, we give the pseudo-code of the enhanced linear CTT-SP algorithm in Figure 6.5. From the pseudo-code, we can see that for a linear DDG with n data sets, we have to add a magnitude of n^2 edges to construct the CTT (lines 1−2). In this enhanced linear CTT-SP algorithm, before actually creating an edge (line 9), we check whether this edge can satisfy the condition of users' tolerance of a regeneration time delay (lines 3−8). Next, we calculate the weight of the edges (lines 10−17), where we add the users' preference attribute λ (line 16). For the longest edge, the complexity of calculating its weight is $O(n^2)$

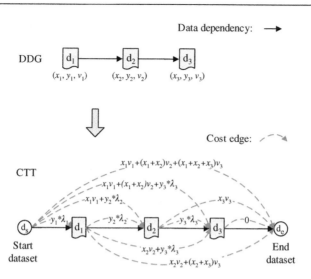

Figure 6.4 An example of constructing CTT by the enhanced CTT-SP algorithm.

Algorithm:	**Enhanced Linear CTT-SP**	
Input:	start dataset d_s; end dataset d_e;	
	a linear DDG;	//Including d_s and d_e
Output:	S;	//MCSS of the DDG
	SCR;	//Minimum cost benchmark

```
01.  for ( every dataset dᵢ in DDG )              //Create CTT
02.      for ( every dataset dⱼ, where  dᵢ → dⱼ )
03.          genCost = 0;
04.          for (every dataset dᵤ, where  dᵢ → dᵤ → dⱼ)
05.              genCost = genCost + xᵤ ;
06.          if ( genCost/Priceₒₚᵤ > Tⱼ₋₁ )
07.              break for;
08.          else
09.              Create e < dᵢ, dⱼ >;            //Create an edge
10.              weight = 0;
11.              for (every dataset dₖ, where  dᵢ → dₖ → dⱼ)
12.                  genCost = 0;
13.                  for (every dataset dₕ, where  dᵢ → dₕ → dₖ)
14.                      genCost = genCost + xₕ ;
15.                  weight = weight + (xₖ + genCost)* vₖ ;
16.              weight = weight + yⱼ*λⱼ;
17.              Set ω < dᵢ, dⱼ >= weight;       //Set weight to an edge
18.  Pₘᵢₙ<dₛ, dₑ> = Dijkstra_Algorithm ( dₛ, dₑ, CTT );
19.  S = set of datasets that Pₘᵢₙ<dₛ, dₑ> traversed;
20.  SCR = (∑_{dⱼ∈DDG} CostRᵢ)_S ;
21.  Return S, SCR;
```

Figure 6.5 Pseudo-code of enhanced CTT-SP algorithm.

(lines 11−15), so a total of $O(n^4)$. Next, the Dijkstra shortest path algorithm has the time complexity of $O(n^2)$ (line 18). Hence, the enhanced linear CTT-SP algorithm also has a worst-case time complexity of $O(n^4)$, and by adding the two new attributes, the algorithm can find the MCSS of linear DDG that satisfies users' tolerance of computation delay and preferences on storage.

6.3.1.2 Rules in the Strategy

Based on the enhanced linear CTT-SP algorithm, we introduce our local-optimisation-based data set storage strategy. The philosophy is to derive localised minimum costs instead of a global one with low time complexity for the strategy. The strategy contains the following four rules:

1. Given a general DDG, the data sets to be stored first are (a) the ones for which users have no tolerance of computation delay and (b) the ones that users choose to store.
2. Then, the DDG is divided into separate sub-DDGs by the stored data sets. For every sub-DDG, if it is a linear one, we use the enhanced CTT-SP algorithm to find its storage strategy; otherwise, we find the data sets that have multiple direct predecessors or successors, and use these data sets as the partitioning points to divide it into sub-linear DDG segments, as shown in Figure 6.6. Then we use the enhanced linear CTT-SP algorithm to find their storage strategies. This is the essence of local optimisation.
3. When new data sets are generated in the system, they will be treated as a new sub-DDG and added to the old DDG. Correspondingly, its storage status will be calculated in the same way as for the old DDG.
4. When a data set's usage rate is changed (by either a system administrator or users), we will recalculate the storage status of the sub-linear DDG that contains this data set.

In the strategy introduced above, the computation time complexity is well controlled within $O(m * n_l^4)$ by dividing the general DDG into sub-linear DDG segments, where m is the number of the sub-linear DDGs and n_l is the number of data sets in the sub-linear DDG segments. Hence our strategy has a very reasonable computation complexity at run-time of the system which depends on the size of the sub-linear DDGs. The efficiency of running the strategy will be evaluated in Section 7.3.2. Meanwhile, by utilising the CTT-SP algorithm, we guarantee that every sub-linear DDG segment in the general DDG is stored with its MCSS, hence achieving the local optimisation.

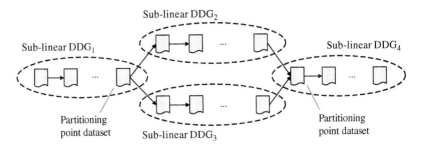

Figure 6.6 Dividing a DDG into sub-linear DDGs.

6.3.2 Cost-Effectiveness Analysis

To analyse the cost-effectiveness of the local-optimisation-based storage strategy, we need the following theorem.

Theorem 6.2 *In a given DDG, assume that S is the MCSS of the DDG. If $d_p \in S$ and d_p divides the DDG into:*

$$\begin{cases} DDG_1 = \{d_j | d_j \in DDG \land d_j \rightarrow d_p\} \\ DDG_2 = \{d_k | d_k \in DDG \land d_p \rightarrow d_k\} \end{cases}$$

then S_1 and S_2 are the MCSSs of DDG_1 and DDG_2, respectively, where $S_1 = S \cap DDG_1$ and $S_2 = S \cap DDG_2$.

Based on Theorem 6.2, we analyse the difference between the cost rate of merging two linear DDG segments together with our strategy and the minimum cost rate (i.e. the benchmark addressed in Chapter 5).

Assume that linear DDG_1 with data sets $\{d_1, d_2, \ldots, d_u\}$ is stored with the minimum cost strategy S_1, which is calculated by the CTT-SP algorithm, and linear DDG_2 with data sets $\{d'_1, d'_2, \ldots, d'_v\}$ is added after DDG_1, as shown in Figure 6.7. We assume that S is the MCSS of the merged DDG.

According to the local-optimisation-based strategy, we calculate the storage strategy S_2 of DDG_2 separately, also by the CTT-SP algorithm. There are two situations as follows:

1. If the last data set d_u in DDG_1 is a stored data set, the cost rate of the two merged DDGs in our strategy is the minimum cost rate, where

$$\left(\sum_{d_i \in DDG_1} CostR_i \right)_{S_1} + \left(\sum_{d_i \in DDG_2} CostR_i \right)_{S_2} = \left(\sum_{d_i \in DDG_1 \cup DDG_2} CostR_i \right)_{S}$$

This can be proved by direct utilisation of the definition of SCR (Formula (4.4) in Section 4.3). Hence, the local-optimisation-based strategy is the MCSS of the DDG in this situation.

2. If the last data set d_u in DDG_1 is a deleted data set, as shown in Figure 6.7, the CTT-SP algorithm on DDG_2 will start from d_k, which is the last stored data set in DDG_1. Hence we have the MCSS S'_2 of the set of data sets after d_k, which is

$$DDG'_2 = \{d_i | d_i \in (DDG_1 \cup DDG_2) \land d_k \rightarrow d_i\}$$

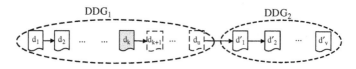

Figure 6.7 Two merging DDG_LS.

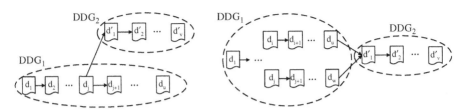

Figure 6.8 Two more scenarios of merging linear DDGs.

Because DDG_1 is stored with the minimum cost strategy and d_k is a stored data set, from Theorem 6.2, we can get S'_1, which is the MCSS of the set of data sets before d_k, which is

$$DDG'_1 = \{d_i | d_i \in DDG_1 \wedge d_i \rightarrow d_k\}$$

Hence, the difference between the cost rate of our strategy and the minimum cost strategy of the merged DDG is:

$$\left(\sum_{d_i \in DDG'_1} CostR_i\right)_{S'_1} + y_k + \left(\sum_{d_i \in DDG'_2} CostR_i\right)_{S'_2} - \left(\sum_{d_i \in DDG_1 \cup DDG_2} CostR_i\right)_S$$
$$< y_k - (CostR_k)_S$$

This is because S'_1 and S'_2 are the minimum cost strategies of DDG'_1 and DDG'_2. Furthermore, since d_k is a deleted data set according to the minimum cost strategy S of the merged DDG (if d_k is a stored data set, then $S'_1 \cup S'_2 = S$ according to Theorem 6.2), we can conclude that the difference between the cost rate of our strategy and the minimum cost strategy is less than

$$y_k - genCost(d_k) * v_k$$

For more complex scenarios of merging DDGs in our strategy, as indicated in Figure 6.8, we have similar conclusions. In Section 7.3.1, we will use experiment results to further demonstrate the cost-effectiveness of the local-optimisation-based storage strategy.

6.4 Summary

In this chapter, we present two novel data set storage strategies that can be facilitated at run-time in the cloud. Besides taking into consideration users' tolerance of computation delays and preferences concerning the storage of some data sets at higher cost, the two strategies provide different levels of efficiency and cost-effectiveness to meet the requirements of different applications. Specifically, the cost-rate-based strategy is highly efficient with fairly reasonable cost-effectiveness, and the local-optimisation-based strategy is highly cost-effective with very reasonable efficiency.

7 Experiments and Evaluations

In this chapter, we evaluate the proposed benchmarking approaches and storage strategies by means of experiments on our SwinCloud environment [60]. In Section 7.1, we introduce SwinCloud, which is a private cloud in Swinburne University of Technology. In Sections 7.2 and 7.3, we conduct general random experiments to evaluate the overall performance of our benchmarking approaches and storage strategies presented in Chapters 5 and 6 respectively. In Section 7.4, we describe a specific case study of the real-world pulsar searching application which is the motivating example described in Section 3.1, in which our benchmarking approaches and storage strategies are illustrated.

7.1 Experiment Environment

SwinCloud is a cloud computing simulation environment. The architecture of SwinCloud is shown in Figure 7.1. It is built on the computing facilities at Swinburne University of Technology and takes advantage of the existing SwinGrid systems [85]. For example, the Swinburne Astrophysics Supercomputer Node (http://astronomy.swin.edu.au/supercomputing/) comprises 145 Dell Power Edge 1950, each with two quad-core Clovertown processors at 2.33 GHz (each processor is a 64-bit low-volt Intel Xeon 5138), 16 GB RAM and 2 × 500 GB drives. We install VMWare [6] on SwinGrid, so that it can offer unified computing and storage resources. Utilising the unified resources, we set up data centres that can host applications. In the data centres, Hadoop [3] is installed, which can facilitate the Map-Reduce [32] computing paradigm and distributed data management.

7.2 Evaluation of Minimum Cost Benchmarking Approaches

In this section, we evaluate the minimum cost benchmarking approaches proposed in Chapter 5 by conducting general random simulations on SwinCloud. In Section 7.2.1, we evaluate the cost-effectiveness of the minimum cost benchmark by comparing it with some intuitive storage strategies. In Section 7.2.2, we evaluate the efficiency of the two different benchmarking approaches.

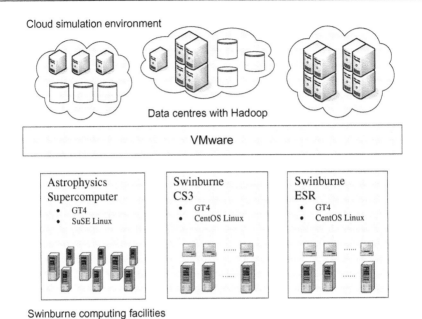

Cloud simulation environment

Data centres with Hadoop

Figure 7.1 SwinCloud infrastructure.

7.2.1 Cost-Effectiveness Evaluation of the Minimum Cost Benchmark

To evaluate the cost-effectiveness of the minimum cost benchmark, we compare it with some representative and intuitive storage strategies, which are as follows:

1. Store none data set: delete all the generated data sets in the cloud, and regenerate them whenever needed.
2. Store all data sets: store all the application data sets in the cloud.
3. Generation-cost-based strategy: store the data sets that incur the highest generation costs.
4. Usage-based strategy: store the data sets that are most frequently used.

For evaluation, we generate random DDGs and derive the minimum cost benchmark via the benchmarking approaches. We run the above four strategies on the DDG and compare the application costs with the minimum cost benchmark. From the large number of test cases in our experiment, we choose and present one as the representative in this sub-section.

In this case, we use a DDG with 50 data sets, each with a random size ranging from 100 GB to 1 TB. The data set generation time is also random, ranging from 1 to 10 h. The usage frequency is again random, ranging from once per day to once per 10 days. The prices of cloud services follow Amazon's cloud cost model, i.e. US$0.1 per CPU instance-hour for computation and US$0.15 per gigabyte per month for storage. We run our benchmarking algorithm on this DDG to calculate the MCSS and the minimum cost benchmark, where 9 of the 50 data sets are

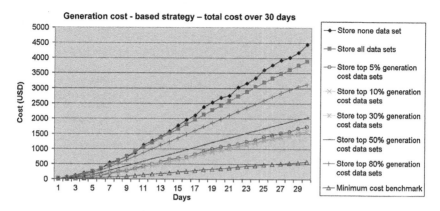

Figure 7.2 Cost-effectiveness evaluation by comparing with the generation-cost-based strategy.

chosen to be stored. We evaluate this minimum cost benchmark by comparing the total application cost of the other storage strategies introduced above.

Figure 7.2 shows the comparison of the minimum cost benchmark with the generation-cost-based strategy. We compare the total application costs over 30 days for the strategies that store different percentages of data sets based on the generation cost and the minimum cost benchmark. The two extreme strategies of storing all the data sets and deleting all the data sets are also included. In Figure 7.2, we can clearly see the cost-effectiveness of different strategies compared with the benchmark. In this case, storing top 10% data sets with highest generation cost turns out to be the most cost-effective strategy, which is still much higher (about 170%) than the minimum cost benchmark.

Then, we compare the minimum cost benchmark with the usage-based strategy. We still run simulations of strategies for storing different percentages of data sets based on their usage frequencies. Figure 7.3 shows the comparison of the total application costs over 30 days, where we can clearly see the cost-effectiveness of different strategies comparing with the benchmark. Also, the strategy of storing top 10% data sets with highest usage frequency turns out to be the most cost-effective one in this case. Compared to Figure 7.2, although the usage-based strategy is more cost-effective than the generation-cost-based strategy, it is again still much higher (about 70%) than the minimum cost benchmark.

From the experiments above, we can see the cost-effectiveness of the minimum cost benchmark, which serves very well as the benchmark for evaluating any storage strategies.

7.2.2 Efficiency Evaluation of Two Benchmarking Approaches

In Chapter 5, we develop two different benchmarking approaches according to different users' requirements, namely the static on-demand approach and the dynamic

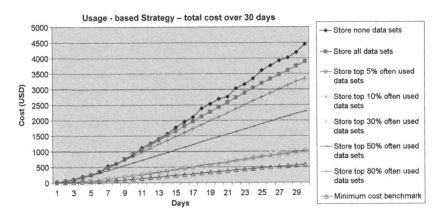

Figure 7.3 Cost-effectiveness evaluation by comparing with the usage-based strategy.

on-the-fly approach. In this sub-section, we evaluate the efficiency of these two approaches.

In the simulation, the same random parameters in Section 7.2.1 are used to generate the DDG_LS with 50 data sets. The prices of cloud services again follow Amazon's cloud cost model. To evaluate the two approaches, we start with one DDG_LS and gradually add new DDG_LSs to it (i.e. from $m = 1$ to $m = 20$). For the DDGs with different sizes, we calculate the updated benchmark of the whole DDG with both the static on-demand benchmarking approach and the dynamic on-the-fly benchmarking approach. Figure 7.4 shows the comparison of CPU time consumed by the two benchmarking approaches.

From Figure 7.4 we can see that the on-demand benchmarking approach is not efficient to keep the minimum cost benchmark updated at runtime. The computation time increases dramatically as the data sets number increases. This is because whenever the cost is changed in the cloud, because of either the generation of new data sets or changes in the existing data sets' usage frequencies, we need to call the CTT-SP algorithm (see Section 5.1.3) for the whole DDG to calculate the new minimum cost benchmark. In contrast, for the dynamic benchmarking approach, as we can see from the zoom-in chart (bottom plane) in Figure 7.4, the time for calculating a new minimum cost benchmark is in the magnitude of seconds in general, hence much more efficient. This is because we take advantage of the pre-calculated PSSs that are saved in the hierarchy (see Section 5.2.4) and only need to recalculate the PSS of the local DDG_LS to derive the new benchmark. Hence the complexity of calculating the new benchmark is more or less independent of the size of the DDG.

More specifically, the zoom-in chart (bottom plane) in Figure 7.4 shows that the time for calculating a new minimum cost benchmark in the case of data sets' usage frequencies changing is less than for the generation of new data sets. This is because when new data sets are generated, we need to create a new CTT for them to calculate the new PSS, whereas when existing data sets' usage frequencies

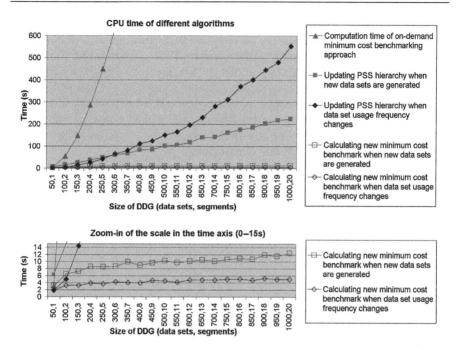

Figure 7.4 Efficiency comparison of two benchmarking approaches.

change in a DDG_LS, we only need to update the weights of the changed edges in the existing CTT instead of creating a new one to recalculate the PSS.

From Figure 7.4, we also note that after the calculation of a new benchmark, the update of the PSS hierarchy takes some computation time. More specifically, the computation time for updating the PSS hierarchy for new data sets' generation increases in a linear manner as the number of DDG_LS grows because we need to add a new PSS to every level of the PSS hierarchy, where the number of levels equals the number of segments in the whole DDG as presented in Section 5.2.4.2. However, in the case of data sets' usage frequencies changing, the computation time increases faster than the case of new data sets' generation. This is because the newly generated data sets have only preceding data sets in the original DDG, while the corresponding DDG_LS of the data sets whose usage frequencies are changed has both preceding and succeeding data sets in the original DDG. According to the rules of updating the PSS hierarchy presented in Section 5.2.4.2 (see Figure 5.25), we have to recalculate more than one PSS in every level of the hierarchy in the case of data sets' usage frequencies changing.

Next, we conduct more specific experiments to analyse the impact on the efficiency of the benchmarking approaches. For the static on-demand approach, the efficiency depends on the number of data sets in the DDG, which is already shown in Figure 7.4. Hence, we mainly investigate the dynamic on-the-fly approach.

PSS is the basis of the dynamic on-the-fly approach, where the efficiency of calculating PSSs plays a decisive role in the overall performance. As discussed in Section 5.2.3.2, the time complexity of calculating PSS is determined by the number of dimensions of the PSS and the number of MCSSs in the PSS. The number of dimensions of a PSS only depends on the structure of the DDG, whereas the number of MCSSs in a PSS may depend on more factors. Hence we mainly investigate the latter, i.e. which factors impact the MCSSs in PSS and how they impact the efficiency of calculating PSS. We also briefly analyse the impact of PSSs' dimensions on efficiency at the end of this sub-section.

Figure 7.5 contains the number of MCSSs in the PSSs generated by the experiments shown in Figure 7.4, where Figure 7.5A shows that as the size of DDG increases, the number of MCSSs in its PSS does not increase in general, and Figure 7.5B further shows eight MCSSs in the PSS of a DDG_LS with 50 data sets in detail. From the figure we can see that the number of MCSSs in the PSS is not correlated to and is much smaller than the number of data sets in the DDG_LSs. This important fact guarantees the efficiency of the on-the-fly benchmarking approach, which is based on the algorithm of calculating PSSs.

Next in the following experiments, we investigate the parameters of the DDG that impact the number of MCSSs in the PSS and their impacts on the efficiency of

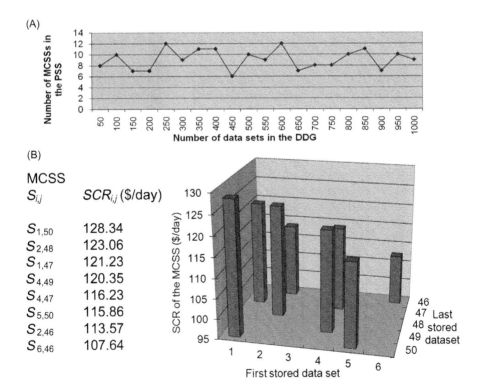

Figure 7.5 MCSSs in PSS.

calculating the PSS. First, we investigate the data sets' generation time. To demonstrate the impact, for every data set in a DDG_LS, we multiply its generation time by a modification parameter (i.e. $0.5 \sim 2$), which changes the generation time from half to double its original value, with other parameters unchanged. With different modification parameters, we generate different modified DDG_LSs and calculate their PSSs. Figure 7.6A demonstrates the number of MCSSs in the PSSs and corresponding CPU times of the calculation, where we can see that as the modification parameter increases (i.e. the generation time of data sets increases), the number of MCSSs in the PSS decreases. Furthermore, because of the fact that the smaller the data sets' generation time, the more data sets in the DDG_LS will be stored to reduce the total application cost. Therefore, we conclude that the more data sets in DDG_LS are stored, the fewer MCSSs are in the PSS. Figure 7.6A also shows that as the number of MCSSs changes, the CPU time of calculating PSS does not change very much. Next we investigate the data sets' sizes and usage frequencies to see their impacts on the PSS. With same experiments for Figure 7.6A, we get similar results which are shown in Figure 7.6B and C. Based on these experiments

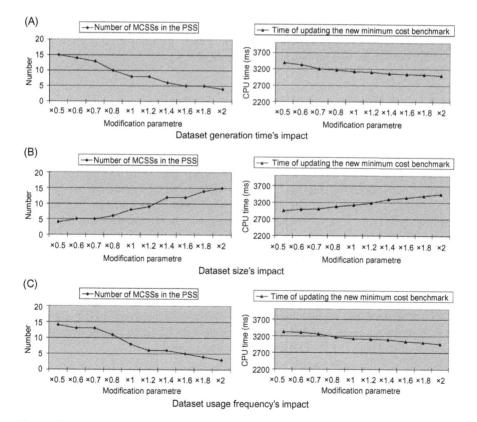

Figure 7.6 Impacts of DDG's parameters on the performance of the dynamic on-the-fly benchmarking approach.

we can see that for randomly generated DDG_LSs with different parameters, the PSSs can be efficiently calculated where the change of the parameters has limited impact on the efficiency of our approach.

Another factor that may impact the efficiency of calculating PSS is the number of dimensions of the PSS. As discussed in Section 5.2.3.2, the impact on time complexity of the PSS dimension number is in the same magnitude as the MCSSs number in the PSS (i.e. $O(n_d^3)$). Furthermore, in real applications the number of dimensions of the PSS (i.e. the branches in the DDG) is usually not very high. Hence the efficiency impact on the PSS calculation is not significant. In Section 7.4, we will utilise our benchmarking approaches in a pulsar searching application that has a DDG_LS.

7.3   Evaluation of Cost-Effective Storage Strategies

In this section, we evaluate the two cost-effective storage strategies proposed in Chapter 6, namely the cost-rate-based strategy and the local-optimisation-based strategy. In Section 7.3.1, we evaluate the cost-effectiveness of the two strategies by comparing them to the minimum cost benchmark. In Section 7.3.2, we evaluate the efficiency of the two proposed storage strategies.

7.3.1   Cost-Effectiveness of Two Storage Strategies

To be consistent, we use the same DDG randomly generated with the parameters in Section 7.2.1 to conduct the experiment. We run the cost-rate-based strategy and local-optimisation-based strategy on the DDG_LS with 50 data sets, and compare the application cost with the minimum cost benchmark and the intuitive storage strategies introduced in Section 7.2.1. To demonstrate the cost-effectiveness of the strategies compared to the minimum cost benchmark, we do not initially consider users' tolerance of computation delay and storage preference. Figure 7.7 shows the comparison of total application cost over 30 days.

From Figure 7.7 we can see that the cost-rate-based strategy is more cost-effective than the generation-cost-based strategy and usage-based strategy for storing the DDG_LS. The local-optimisation-based strategy stores the data sets with the same cost with the minimum cost benchmark. This is because we treat the DDG_LS as the entire segment and directly utilise the enhanced CTT-SP algorithm on it. Next we do more simulations on larger general DDGs to further demonstrate the cost-effectiveness of the two proposed storage strategies.

We still use the same random parameters to generate the DDG_LS with 50 data sets. In the same way as Section 7.2.2, we start from one DDG_LS and gradually add new DDG_LSs to it. Hence for the local-optimisation-based strategy, every DDG_LS is a segment to utilise the enhanced CTT-SP algorithm. In contrast with the former simulations, we no longer accumulate the total cost; instead, we calculate the cost rate (average daily cost over 30 days) of storing all the data sets. This

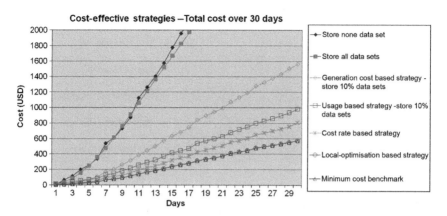

Figure 7.7 Comparison of the total cost for different storage strategies.

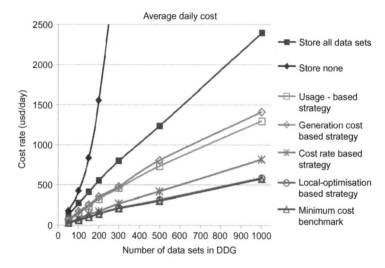

Figure 7.8 Comparison of the cost rate for different storage strategies.

allows us to incorporate more simulation results in one figure for the purpose of better comparison. The results are shown in Figure 7.8.

Figure 7.8 shows the increases of the cost rates of different strategies as the number of data sets grows in the DDG. The results are consistent with formal experiments, where we can see the 'store none' and 'store all' strategies are very cost-ineffective because their cost rates grow fast as the number of data sets grows. The cost-rate-based strategy is better than both the generation-cost-based strategy

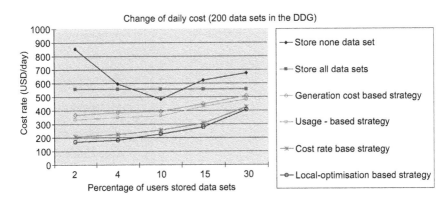

Figure 7.9 Impact on cost-effectiveness of the storage strategies.

and usage-based strategy. The local-optimisation-based strategy is the most cost-effective data sets storage strategy, which is very close to the minimum cost benchmark. Hence the local-optimisation-based strategy is highly cost-effective.

As discussed in Section 6.1, cost is not the only issue for storing application data sets in the cloud, and users may have a certain degree of tolerance for data accessing delay and prefer to store some data sets at a higher cost. The storage of these data sets may well incur extra application cost, which has some impact on the cost-effectiveness of the storage strategies. The more data sets users choose to store, the fewer data sets the storage strategy can apply to; hence the data sets storage strategy would become less cost-effective. Next, we ran another set of simulations on a 200-data sets DDG with different percentages of the data sets stored in the cloud based on users' preferences rather than cost. The rest of the parameter setting is the same as previous simulations. The results are shown in Figure 7.9.

From Figure 7.9 we can see that besides the two extreme strategies, i.e. store none data set and store all the data sets, the remaining four strategies gradually become more cost-ineffective as the percentage of users' stored data sets increases. However, the cost-rate-based strategy and local-optimisation-based strategy proposed in this book are still more cost-effective than others.

7.3.2 Efficiency Evaluation of Two Storage Strategies

The storage strategies are designed for runtime utilisation in the cloud, so they need to be efficient. In this sub-section, we evaluate the efficiency of the two proposed strategies by comparing their execution time to the original CTT-SP algorithm used for benchmarking and the intuitive storage strategies.

In the simulations, we assume that a DDG with 200 data sets is stored in the cloud and, in the DDG, segments with different numbers of data sets are newly generated or their usage frequencies are changed. We recalculate the storage status

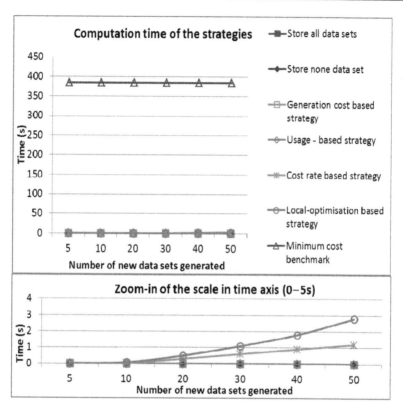

Figure 7.10 Efficiency comparisons of different storage strategies for a 200-data set DDG.

of the DDG using different storage strategies and their computation times are shown in Figure 7.10.

As we can see from Figure 7.10, the computation time of the minimum cost benchmarking approach is far higher than that of other storage strategies and is, in fact, impractical at runtime, e.g. taking more than 6 min for this case and increasing very rapidly when the number of data sets grows. This is because its computation complexity depends on the total number of data sets, which means that for any number of newly generated data sets or changes of the data sets' usage frequencies, we need to call the general CTT-SP algorithm (i.e. with the time complexity of $O(n^9)$ [90]) on the whole DDG to find the minimum cost storage strategy. Hence it can only be used for on-demand benchmarking.

Furthermore, in the zoomed chart at the bottom of Figure 7.10, the computation time of the 'store all data sets' strategy, the 'store none data set' strategy, the generation-cost-based strategy and the usage-based strategy are all zero. This is because they are static strategies where all the data sets' storage statuses are pre-defined. Hence they do not involve extra runtime computation. For our cost-effective storage strategies, they are also very efficient as depicted in the zoomed chart, although some runtime computation is involved. The cost-rate-based strategy is highly efficient. Although the local-optimisation-based strategy is not as efficient as the cost-rate-based strategy, we still deem it practical for runtime utilisation. For example, for the segment with 50 data sets (either newly generated or with usage frequencies changed), our strategy takes less than 3 s.

7.4   Case Study of Pulsar Searching Application

As introduced in Section 3.1, pulsar searching is a typical scientific application in astrophysics. In this section, we demonstrate how the pulsar case utilises our benchmarking approaches and storage strategies for storing the generated application data sets.

In the pulsar case, during the workflow's execution on analysing just *one piece* of the observation data, six data sets are generated. The DDG of these data sets is shown in Figure 7.11, as well as the sizes and generation times of these data sets. From the Swinburne astrophysics research group, we understand that the 'de-dispersion files' are the most useful generated data set. Based on these files, many accelerating and seeking methods can be used to search for pulsar candidates. Based on the scenario, we set the 'de-dispersion files' to be used once every four days, and the rest of the data sets to be used once every 10 days. Furthermore, we also assume that the prices of cloud services follow Amazon's cloud cost model.

7.4.1   Utilisation of Minimum Cost Benchmarking Approaches

The utilisation of the static on-demand benchmarking approach is straightforward. We directly create the CTT on the DDG and find the MCSS, which is storing d_2, d_4, d_6 and deleting d_1, d_3, d_5. The minimum cost benchmark is US\$0.51 per day.

Next, we demonstrate the utilisation of the dynamic on-the-fly benchmarking approach. As described in Section 3.1, there are two phases in execution of the workflow to generate the DDG: *Files Preparation* and *Seeking Candidates*, where in each phase three data sets are generated as a DDG_LS. Figure 7.12 demonstrates the PSS calculation of the two DDG_LSs and the merging process for the PSS of the whole DDG segment.

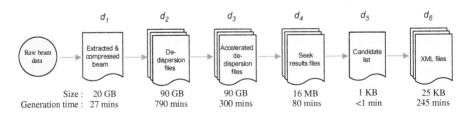

Figure 7.11 DDG of pulsar searching application.

When data sets d_1, d_2, d_3 are generated as DDG_LS_1, we calculate PSS_1. Next, when data sets d_4, d_5, d_6 are generated as DDG_LS_2, we first calculate its PSS, denoted as PSS_2, then we locate the corresponding MCSS from PSS_1 and form the MCSS of the whole DDG segment which stores data sets d_2, d_4, d_6. Next, we calculate the cost rate of the MCSS, which is again US\$0.51 per day for storing these six data sets. This cost rate is the minimum cost benchmark. After we derive the new benchmark, we need to merge PSS_1 and PSS_2 to derive the PSS of the whole DDG segment, which is saved in the hierarchy for further use.

7.4.2 Utilisation of Cost-Effective Storage Strategies

The storage strategies are utilised at runtime in the cloud. As time goes on, researchers may reuse the data sets and conduct new re-analysis on them, where new data sets are generated. Based on the scenario, we set that new data sets are

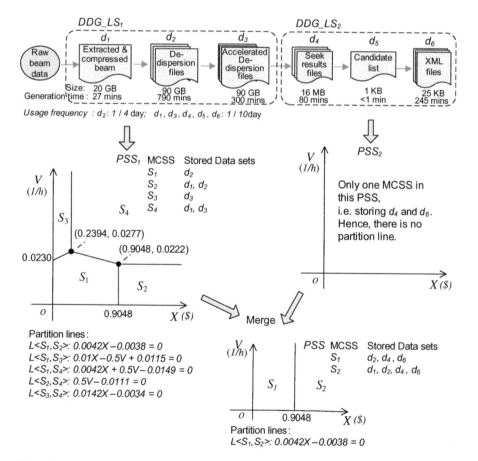

Figure 7.12 PSSs of a DDG segment in the pulsar application.

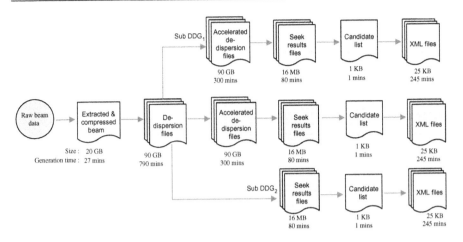

Figure 7.13 DDG of the pulsar application with new data sets' generation.

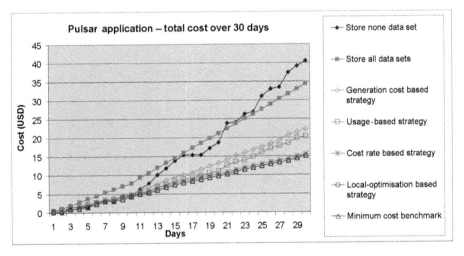

Figure 7.14 Cost-effectiveness comparisons of different storage strategies for storing pulsar case DDG.

generated on the 10th day and 20th day, indicated as sub-DDG_1 and sub-DDG_2 in Figure 7.13.

We run the two proposed cost-effective storage strategies on the DDG and compare the total application cost with the same storage strategies previously presented and the minimum cost benchmark. The simulation results are shown in Figure 7.14.

From Figure 7.14 we can see that (1) the cost of the 'store none data set' strategy is a fluctuating line because in this strategy all the costs are computation cost of regenerating data sets. For the days that have fewer requests for data, the cost is

Table 7.1 Storage Status of Data Sets in the Pulsar Application with Different Storage Strategies

Data Sets/ Strategies	Extracted Beam	De-dispersion Files	Accelerated De-dispersion Files	Seek Results	Pulsar Candidates	XML Files
(1) Store none data set	Deleted	Deleted	Deleted	Deleted	Deleted	Deleted
(2) Store all data sets	Stored	Stored	Stored	Stored	Stored	Stored
(3) Generation-cost-based strategy	Deleted	Stored	Stored	Deleted	Deleted	Stored
(4) Usage-based strategy	Deleted	Stored	Deleted	Deleted	Deleted	Deleted
(5) Cost-rate-based strategy	Deleted	Stored (deleted initially)	Deleted	Stored	Deleted	Stored
(6) Local-optimisation-based strategy	Deleted	Stored	Deleted	Stored	Deleted	Stored
(7) Minimum cost benchmark	Deleted	Stored	Deleted	Stored	Deleted	Stored

low; otherwise, the cost is high; (2) the cost of the 'store all data sets' strategy is a polyline, because all the data sets are stored in the system that is charged at a fixed rate, and the inflection points only occur when new data sets are generated; (3–4) the costs of the generation-cost-based strategy and the usage-based strategy are in the middle band and are lower than the 'store none data set' and 'store all data sets' storage strategies. The cost lines are slightly fluctuated because the data sets are partially stored; (5–6) the cost-rate-based strategy has a good performance and the most cost-effective data sets storage strategy is the local-optimisation-based strategy which achieves storage of the data sets with the minimum cost in this pulsar searching application. Table 7.1 shows how the data sets are stored with different strategies in detail.

Since the pulsar DDG shown in Figure 7.13 is not complicated, we can do some intuitive analyses on how to store the generated data sets. For the data set of *accelerated de-dispersion files*, although its generation cost is quite high compared to its huge size, it is not worth storing them in the cloud. However, in the generation-cost-based strategy, these files are stored. In the case of the final *XML files*, these are not very often used, but compared to their high generation cost and small size, they should be stored. However, in the usage-based strategy, these files are not stored. For the data set of *de-dispersion files*, by comparing its own generation cost rate and storage cost rate, the cost-rate-based strategy did not store it at the beginning, but did store it after it was used in the regeneration of other data sets. In this case the local-optimisation-based strategy is the most cost-effective data sets storage strategy and achieves the minimum cost storage strategy.

7.5 Summary

In this chapter, we demonstrate the experiment results that we conducted on our SwinCloud environment to evaluate the proposed minimum cost benchmarking approaches and cost-effective data sets storage strategies presented in this book.

For the minimum cost benchmarking approaches, first, by comparing with some intuitive storage strategies, we demonstrate the cost-effectiveness of the minimum cost benchmark, and then by comparing the runtime efficiency of the two proposed approaches, i.e. static on-demand approach and dynamic on-the-fly approach, we further demonstrate that two approaches are suitable for different applications with different requirements of benchmarking requests.

For the cost-effective data sets storage strategies, we compare them with the minimum cost benchmark to evaluate their cost-effectiveness. Then we evaluate the efficiency of the strategies by comparing their execution time with the benchmarking approaches. The experiment results indicate that the two proposed strategies have different features: the cost-rate-based strategy is highly efficient with fairly reasonable cost-effectiveness and the local-optimisation-based strategy is highly cost-effective with very reasonable efficiency. They can be utilised in different situations according to the requirements of the applications.

At last, we present the case study conducted on the pulsar searching application in astrophysics. By utilising our benchmarking approaches and storage strategies in this real-world application, we successfully demonstrate the practicability of our research.

8 Conclusions and Contributions

In this chapter, we summarise the whole book. Section 8.1 summarises the contents of the whole book. Section 8.2 outlines the main contributions of this book.

8.1 Summary of This Book

The research objective described in this book is to investigate the issue of computation and storage trade-off in the cloud in order to help both users and service providers to bring the cost down dramatically when deploying the computation and data-intensive scientific applications with the pay-as-you-go model. This book was organised as follows:

- Chapter 1 introduced the scientific applications in the cloud, which is the background of this research. Chapter 1 also described the aims of this work, the key issues to be addressed in this book and the primary structure of this book.
- Chapter 2 overviewed the related literature on scientific applications in grid and cloud systems and analysed their limitations. Specifically first we overviewed the data management of scientific applications in traditional distributed systems, e.g. grid systems. Next we reviewed some related work on deploying scientific applications in the cloud and demonstrated the cost-effectiveness of using the cloud. Furthermore, we pointed out that this research is a step forward based on the existing work, which investigates how to reduce the application cost in the cloud.
- Chapter 3 presented a motivating example of pulsar searching from astrophysics. Based on the example, we analysed the problems of deploying scientific applications in the cloud and defined the scope of this research. Based on the analysis, we presented the detailed research issues of this book: (i) the cost model for data sets storage in the cloud, (ii) minimum cost benchmarking approaches, and (iii) cost-effective data sets storage strategies.
- Chapter 4 described a new cost model for data sets storage in the cloud. First, we introduced a classification of the application data in the cloud, namely original data and generated data, and proposed the important concept of the DDG. Then, we presented the cost model for data sets storage based on DDG, where the total application cost defined in this book is the sum of the computation cost for regenerating data sets and the storage cost for generated data sets. The cost model represents the trade-off between computation and storage, which was investigated in this book to reduce the application cost in the cloud.
- Chapter 5 described two novel minimum cost benchmarking approaches. This chapter is the core of this book, because benchmarking is to calculate the minimum cost of storing the application data sets in the cloud, which achieves the best trade-off between

computation and storage. Most of the important theorems and algorithms were presented in this chapter, based on which we proposed two benchmarking approaches (i.e. the static on-demand approach and the dynamic on-the-fly approach) according to the different requirements of applications in the cloud.

• Chapter 6 described two innovative cost-effective data sets storage strategies. By utilising the trade-off between computation and storage, two cost-effective data sets storage strategies were designed according to the different requirements of applications in the cloud, i.e. the cost-rate-based strategy (highly efficient with fairly reasonable cost-effectiveness) and the local-optimisation-based strategy (highly cost-effective with very reasonable efficiency).

• Chapter 7 described the experiments and evaluations of this research. First, general random experiments demonstrated that the minimum cost benchmarking approaches can very well evaluate the cost-effectiveness of storage strategies, and the proposed cost-effective storage strategies can also be utilised in different situations according to different application requirements in the cloud. Then, the case study on the specific pulsar searching application further demonstrated the practicability of our benchmarking approaches and storage strategies.

In summary, wrapping up all the chapters, we can conclude that with the research results in this book, i.e. cost model, benchmarking approaches and storage strategies, the application cost in the cloud can be significantly reduced.

8.2   Key Contributions of This Book

The significance of this research is that we have investigated a brand-new and niche issue in cloud computing, i.e. the trade-off between computation and storage of data in scientific applications. Because of the wide utilisation of the pay-as-you-go model, application cost becomes an important issue when deploying applications in the cloud. This book provides a novel way to reduce the application cost via achieving the best trade-off of computation and storage in the cloud.

In particular the major contributions of this book are as follows:

1. For the first time, the issue of computation and storage trade-off for scientific data sets storage in the cloud is comprehensively and systematically investigated. A brand-new cost model for data sets storage is proposed based on the novel concept of the DDG. This cost model represents the trade-off between computation and storage in the application cost.

2. For the first time, a static on-demand minimum cost benchmarking approach is proposed. In this approach, a novel CTT-SP-based algorithm is designed to calculate the theoretical minimum application cost of storing the generated data sets in the cloud. This algorithm solves a seemingly NP-hard problem in polynomial time complexity, i.e. $O(n^9)$.

3. For the first time, a dynamic on-the-fly minimum cost benchmarking approach is proposed. With in-depth investigation of the trade-off between computation and storage, a novel concept of PSS is proposed. Based on PSS, we develop an innovative approach that can dynamically derive the minimum cost benchmark on the fly at runtime in the cloud.

4. For the first time, a cost-rate-based data sets storage strategy is proposed. This strategy is highly efficient with fairly reasonable cost-effectiveness and contains three new

algorithms to handle all situations (i.e. for new data sets, stored data sets and regenerated data sets) in the cloud to decide the proper storage status of the application data sets.

5. For the first time a local-optimisation-based data sets storage strategy is proposed. This strategy is highly cost-effective with very reasonable efficiency and contains an enhanced CTT-SP algorithm to decide the proper storage status of the application data sets.

6. A case study is conducted on a real-world scientific application, i.e. pulsar searching in astrophysics. All the proposed benchmarking approaches and storage strategies are utilised in the case study, which demonstrates the practicability of the research outcomes presented in this book.

Appendix A

Notation Index

B	A block in a DDG
Br	A branch in a block
$CostR_i$	Cost rate of data set d_i in the DDG
CTT	Cost Transitive Tournament
CTT-SP	Cost Transitive Tournament-based Shortest Path
d_i	A data set, where the subscript i is the index number
DDG	Data Dependency Graph
DDG_LS	Linear DDG Segment
$e < d_i, d_j >$	The edge from d_i to d_j in the CTT
f_i	A flag that denotes whether data set d_i is stored or deleted
$genCost(d_i)$	Generation cost of data set d_i
$L < S_1, S_2 >$	Partition line between MCSSs S_1 and S_2 in a two-dimensional PSS
MB	Main branch of a DDG
MCSS	Minimum Cost Storage Strategy
$P < S_1, S_2 >$	Partition plane between MCSS S_1 and S_2 in a three-dimensional PSS
$P_{min} < d_i, d_j >$	The shortest path from d_i to d_j in the CTT
$Price_{cpu}$	The price of computation resources in the cloud
$provSet_i$	Set of stored provenance data sets that are needed for regenerating d_i
PSS	Partitioned Solution Space
S	A storage strategy which is a set of data sets in the corresponding DDG (or DDG segment)
S_i	A storage strategy of a DDG (or DDG segment), where the subscript i is the index number
$S_{i,...j}$	A storage strategy, where the subscripts $i,...j$ denote the indices of the first and last stored data sets in the DDG segment
S_{max}	The MCSS that has the maximum SCR in the PSS
S_{min}	The MCSS that has the minimum SCR in the PSS
S_All	Set of MCSSs of a DDG segment with SCR values in the valid range
SB	Sub-branch(es) of a DDG
S_ini	Set of MCSSs for the initial input of calculating PSS
SCR	Sum of cost rates of data sets in a DDG (or DDG segment)
SCR_i	The SCR with storage strategy S_i
$SCR_{i,...j}$	The SCR with storage strategy $S_{i,...j}$
T_i	The time duration that denotes user's tolerance of data set accessing d_i's delay
TCR	Total Cost Rate of a DDG segment in the whole DDG

TCR_i	The TCR with storage strategy S_i
$TCR_{i,\ldots,j}$	The TCR with storage strategy $S_{i,\ldots,j}$
v_i	Usage frequency of data set d_i
V	Sum of deleted succeeding data sets' usage frequencies of a DDG_LS
x_i	Generation cost of data set d_i from its direct predecessors
X	Sum of deleted preceding data sets' generation costs of a DDG_LS
y_i	Storage cost rate data set d_i
$\omega < d_i, d_j >$	The weight of edge $e < d_i, d_j >$
λ_i	User's preference of storing data set d_i with a higher storage cost
$\rightarrow$	Denotation of two data sets having a generation relationship
$\leftrightarrow$	Denotation of two data sets not having a generation relationship

Appendix B
Proofs of Theorems, Lemmas and Corollaries

Theorem 5.1 *Given a linear* DDG *with data sets* $\{d_1, d_2, \ldots, d_n\}$, *the length of* $P_{min} < d_s, d_e >$ *of its CTT is the minimum cost rate for storing the data sets in the* DDG, *and the corresponding storage strategy is to store the data sets that* $P_{min} < d_s, d_e >$ *traverses.*

Proof of Theorem 5.1: First, there is a one-to-one mapping between the storage strategies of the DDG and the paths from d_s to d_e in the CTT. Given any storage strategy of the DDG, we can find an order of these stored data sets, since the DDG is linear. Then, we can find the exact path in the CTT that has traversed all these stored data sets. Similarly, given any path from d_s to d_e in the CTT, we can find the data sets it has traversed, which is a storage strategy. Second, based on the setting of weights to the edges, the length of a path from d_s to d_e in the CTT equals the total cost rate of the corresponding storage strategy. Third, $P_{min} < d_s, d_e >$ is the shortest path from d_s to d_e as found by the Dijkstra algorithm.

Theorem 5.1 holds.

Corollary 5.1 *During the process of finding the shortest path, for every data set* d_f *that is discovered by the Dijkstra algorithm, we have a path* $P_{min} < d_s, d_f >$ *from* d_s *to* d_f *and a set of data sets* S_f *that* $P_{min} < d_s, d_f >$ *traverses.* S_f *is the MCSS of the* sub-DDG *segment* $\{d_i | d_i \in DDG \wedge d_s \rightarrow d_i \rightarrow d_f\}$.

Proof of Corollary 5.1: Corollary 5.1 is proved by apagoge.

Suppose that there exists a storage strategy $S_f' \neq S_f$ and S_f' is the MCSS of the sub-DDG segment $\{d_i | d_i \in DDG \wedge d_s \rightarrow d_i \rightarrow d_f\}$. Then we can get a path $P_{min}' < d_s, d_f >$ from d_s to d_f, which traverses the data sets in S_f'. Then we have:

$$P_{min}' < d_s, d_f > = \left(\sum_{d_i \in DDG \wedge d_s \rightarrow d_i \rightarrow d_f} CostR_i \right)_{S_f'}$$
$$< \left(\sum_{d_i \in DDG \wedge d_s \rightarrow d_i \rightarrow d_f} CostR_i \right)_{S_f} = P_{min} < d_s, d_f >$$

This is contradictory to the known condition '$P_{min} < d_s, d_f >$ is the shortest path from d_s to d_f.' Hence, S_f is the MCSS of the sub-DDG segment $\{d_i | d_i \in DDG \wedge d_s \rightarrow d_i \rightarrow d_f\}$.

Corollary 5.1 holds.

Theorem 5.2 *The selection of main branch in the* DDG *to construct* CTT *has no impact on finding the* MCSS.

Proof of Theorem 5.2: Assume that strategy S is the MCSS of a DDG; the DDG has two sub-branches Br_1 and Br_2 in a block; strategies S_1 and S_2 contain the sets of stored data sets of Br_1 and Br_2 in S.

If we select the main branch with the sub-branch Br_1, S can be mapped to a path in one of the created CTTs. According to Theorem 5.1, the paths in CTT have one-to-one mapping to the storage strategies; hence, we can find a path $P < d_s, d_e >$ that traverses the stored data sets in the main branch according to S. If $S_1 = \emptyset$, there is an over-block edge in the path $P < d_s, d_e >$, which contains the MCSS of Br_2 according to formula (5.2), where $P < d_s, d_e >$ is in the initial CTT. If $S_1 \neq \emptyset$, there is an in-block edge and an out-block edge in $P < d_s, d_e >$, denoted as $e < d_i, d_j >$ and $e < d_h, d_k >$. The weight of $e < d_h, d_k >$ contains the MCSS of Br_2 according to formula (5.2); hence, $P < d_s, d_e >$ is in CTT$(e < d_i, d_j >)$. Similar to Theorem 5.1, we can further prove that the length of $P < d_s, d_e >$ equals the total cost rate of the storage strategy S.

Similarly, if we select the main branch with the sub-branch Br_2, S can also be mapped to a path in one of the created CTTs, where the length of the path equals the total cost rate of the MCSS.

Therefore, no matter which branch we select as the main branch to construct CTT, the MCSS always exists in one of the created CTTs. This means that the selection of the main branch has no impact on finding the MCSS.

Theorem 5.2 holds.

Theorem 5.3 *The Dijkstra shortest path algorithm is still applicable to find the* MCSS *of the* DDG *with one block*.

Proof of Theorem 5.3: In the CTTs created for the DDG with one block, every path from d_s to d_e contains an out-block edge or over-block edge. According to formula (5.2), the minimum cost rate of the sub-branch is contained in the weights of out-block and over-block edges. Hence, every path from d_s to d_e in the CTT contains the MCSS of the sub-branch. Furthermore, the CTTs are created based on the main branch of the DDG; similar to the proof of Theorem 5.1, the shortest path $P_{min} < d_s, d_e >$ found by the Dijkstra algorithm contains the MCSS of the main branch. This means that $P_{min} < d_s, d_e >$ represents the MCSS of the whole DDG.

Theorem 5.3 holds.

Theorem 5.4 *For a* DDG_LS, *only the generation cost of its deleted preceding data sets and the usage frequencies of its deleted succeeding data sets impact on its* MCSS.

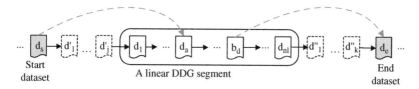

Figure A.1 A DDG_LS with start and end data sets.

Proof of Theorem 5.4: We assume that a DDG_LS $\{d_1, d_2, \ldots, d_{nl}\}$ have j deleted preceding data sets and k deleted succeeding data sets, which is shown in Figure A.1.

In Figure A.1, we can see that the deleted preceding data sets impact on the weights of all the edges from d_s to the DDG_LS. According to the CTT-SP algorithm, for any data set d_a in the DDG_LS, the weight of the edge from d_s to d_a is

$$
\begin{aligned}
w<d_s, d_a> &= y_a + \sum_{\{d_i \mid d_i \in DDG \wedge d_s \rightarrow d_i \rightarrow d_a\}} (genCost(d_i) * v_i) \\
&= y_a + \sum_{i=1}^{j} (genCost(d_i') * v_i') + \sum_{i=1}^{a-1} (genCost(d_i) * v_i) \\
&= y_a + \sum_{i=1}^{j} \left(\left(\sum_{h=1}^{i} x_h' \right) * v_i' \right) + \sum_{i=1}^{a-1} \left(\left(\sum_{h=1}^{j} x_h' + \sum_{h=1}^{i} x_h \right) * v_i \right) \\
&= y_a + \sum_{i=1}^{j} \left(\left(\sum_{h=1}^{i} x_h' \right) * v_i' \right) + \sum_{h=1}^{j} x_h' * \sum_{i=1}^{a-1} v_i + \sum_{i=1}^{a-1} \left(\left(\sum_{h=1}^{i} x_h \right) * v_i \right)
\end{aligned}
$$

From the composition of $w<d_s, d_a>$, we can see that

- $\sum_{i=1}^{j} \left(\left(\sum_{h=1}^{i} x_h' \right) * v_i' \right)$ is a fixed value for all the edges starting from d_s to any data sets in the DDG_LS because it does not contain variable a. Hence, it has no impact on finding the MCSS.
- $\sum_{i=1}^{a-1} \left(\left(\sum_{h=1}^{i} x_h \right) * v_i \right) + y_a$ is a value that is independent of the deleted preceding data sets.
- The value of $\sum_{h=1}^{j} x_h' * \sum_{i=1}^{a-1} v_i$ depends on both the deleted preceding data sets (i.e. $\sum_{h=1}^{j} x_h'$) and the data sets in the DDG_LS (i.e. $\sum_{i=1}^{a-1} v_i$), where $\sum_{h=1}^{j} x_h'$ is the generation cost of the deleted preceding data sets.

Hence, we can come to the conclusion that only the generation costs of the deleted preceding data sets impact on the MCSS of the DDG_LS.

Similarly, for an edge from any data sets d_b in the DDG_LS pointing to d_e, the weight $w<d_b, d_e>$ is

$$
\begin{aligned}
w<d_b, d_e> &= y_e + \sum_{i=b+1}^{nl} \left(\left(\sum_{h=b+1}^{i} x_h \right) * v_i \right) \\
&\quad + \sum_{h=b+1}^{nl} x_h * \sum_{i=1}^{k} v_i'' + \sum_{i=1}^{k} \left(\left(\sum_{h=1}^{i} x_h'' \right) * v_i'' \right)
\end{aligned}
$$

Therefore, only the usage frequencies of the deleted succeeding data sets, i.e. $\sum_{i=1}^{k} v_i''$, impacts on the MCSS of the DDG_LS.

Theorem 5.4 holds.

Theorem 5.5 *Given a* DDG_LS $\{d_1, d_2, \ldots, d_{nl}\}$, SCR_{min} *is the cost rate of* MCSS $S_{u,v}$ *with* $X = 0$, $V = 0$, *and* SCR_{max} *is the cost rate of* MCSS $S_{1,nl}$ *with* $X > y_1/v_1$, $V > y_{nl}/x_{nl}$. *Then we have* $SCR_{min} < SCR_{i,j} < SCR_{max}$, *where* $SCR_{i,j}$ *is the cost rate of* MCSS $S_{i,j}$ *with any given X and V.*

Proof of Theorem 5.5: First, $SCR_{min} < SCR_{i,j}$ is obviously true because of the direct utilisation of the CTT-SP algorithm. Next, we prove $SCR_{i,j} < SCR_{max}$ by apagoge.

We assume $SCR_{i,j} \geq SCR_{max}$, then we have

$$
\begin{aligned}
TCR_{i,j} &= X * \sum_{k=1}^{i-1} v_k + SCR_{i,j} + V * \sum_{k=j+1}^{n_l} x_k \\
&\geq X * \sum_{k=1}^{1-1} v_k + SCR_{max} + V * \sum_{k=n_l+1}^{n_l} x_k > SCR_{max} = TCR_{max}
\end{aligned}
$$

This is contradictory to the known condition that $S_{i,j}$ is the MCSS of the given X and V.

Theorem 5.5 holds.
Lemmas 5.1–5.3 and Theorem 5.6 can be proved in a similar way, which is via the linear equation theory in Linear Algebra.

Lemma 5.1 *In the PSS of a* DDG_LS, *for three MCSSs, if any two of them are adjacent to each other, then the three partition lines between every two MCSSs intersect at one point.*

Proof of Lemma 5.1: For the three lines in Figure 5.15, we can write their equations in the coefficient matrix format, i.e. $Ax = b$, as follows:

$$
A = \begin{bmatrix} \sum_{h=j}^{i-1} v_h & \sum_{h=i'+1}^{j'} x_h \\ \sum_{h=k}^{i-1} v_h & \sum_{h=i'+1}^{k'} x_h \\ -\sum_{h=j}^{k-1} v_h & \sum_{h=j'+1}^{k'} x_h \end{bmatrix}, \quad x = \begin{bmatrix} X \\ V \end{bmatrix}, \quad b = \begin{bmatrix} (SCR_{j,j'} - SCR_{i,i'}) \\ (SCR_{k,k'} - SCR_{i,i'}) \\ (SCR_{k,k'} - SCR_{j,j'}) \end{bmatrix}
$$

Because of $d_j \rightarrow d_k \rightarrow d_i$ and $d_{i'} \rightarrow d_{j'} \rightarrow d_{k'}$, we have $\sum_{h=j}^{k-1} v_h + \sum_{h=k}^{i-1} v_h = \sum_{h=j}^{i-1} v_h$ and $\sum_{h=i'+1}^{j'} x_h - \sum_{h=i'+1}^{k'} x_h = -\sum_{h=j'+1}^{k'} x_h$; hence, in matrix A there are only two linear independent vectors. Hence, the equation system $Ax = b$ has a unique solution.

Hence, the three lines (i.e. $L < S_{i,i'}, S_{j,j'} >$, $L < S_{i,i'}, S_{k,k'} >$ and $L < S_{j,j'}, S_{k,k'} >$) intersect at one point.

Lemma 5.1 holds.

Lemma 5.2 *In a three-dimensional PSS, for three MCSSs, if any two of them are adjacent to each other, then the three partition planes intersect in one line.*

Proof of Lemma 5.2: Similar to the proof of Lemma 5.7, we can write the partition planes' equations in Figure 5.19 in the coefficient matrix format as follows:

$$A = \begin{bmatrix} \sum_{a_1}^{b_1} v & \sum_{a_2}^{b_2} x & \sum_{a_3}^{b_3} x \\ \sum_{b_1}^{c_1} v & \sum_{b_2}^{c_2} x & \sum_{b_3}^{c_3} x \\ \sum_{a_1}^{c_1} v & \sum_{a_2}^{c_2} x & \sum_{a_3}^{c_3} x \end{bmatrix}, \quad x\begin{bmatrix} X_1 \\ V_2 \\ V_3 \end{bmatrix}, \quad b = \begin{bmatrix} (SCR_b - SCR_a) \\ (SCR_c - SCR_b) \\ (SCR_c - SCR_a) \end{bmatrix}$$

Because of $d_{c_1} \rightarrow d_{b_1} \rightarrow d_{a_1}$, $d_{a_2} \rightarrow d_{b_2} \rightarrow d_{c_2}$ and $d_{a_3} \rightarrow d_{b_3} \rightarrow d_{c_3}$, we have $\sum_{a_1}^{b_1} v + \sum_{b_1}^{c_1} v = \sum_{a_1}^{c_1} v$, $\sum_{a_2}^{b_2} x + \sum_{b_2}^{c_2} x = \sum_{a_2}^{c_2} x$ and $\sum_{a_3}^{b_3} x + \sum_{b_3}^{c_3} x = \sum_{a_3}^{c_3} x$; hence, in matrix A there are only two linear independent vectors.

According to the property of three-variable linear equations, the solution space of the equation system $Ax = b$ is a line.

Hence, the three lines (i.e. $P < S_a, S_b >$, $P < S_b, S_c >$ and $P < S_a, S_c >$) intersect in one line.

Lemma 5.2 holds.

Lemma 5.3 *In a three-dimensional PSS, for four MCSSs, if any three of them intersect in a different line, then the four intersection lines intersect at one point.*

Proof of Lemma 5.3: For four MCSSs in a three-dimensional PSS, the maximum number of linear independent vectors in the partition plane equations' coefficient matrix is three. We still take Figure 5.19's DDG segment as our example. We assume that S_e is the fourth MCSS, where $SCR_a < SCR_b < SCR_c < SCR_e$; $d_{e_1} \rightarrow d_{c_1} \rightarrow d_{b_1} \rightarrow d_{a_1}$, $d_{a_2} \rightarrow d_{b_2} \rightarrow d_{c_2} \rightarrow d_{e_2}$, and $d_{a_3} \rightarrow d_{b_3} \rightarrow d_{c_3} \rightarrow d_{e_3}$. We have partition plane equations of the four MCSSs as follows:

$$P<S_a,S_b>: \left(\sum_{a_1}^{b_1} v\right)*X_1 + \left(\sum_{a_2}^{b_2} x\right)*V_2 + \left(\sum_{a_3}^{b_3} x\right)*V_3 = SCR_b - SCR_a$$

$$P<S_a,S_c>: \left(\sum_{a_1}^{c_1} v\right)*X_1 + \left(\sum_{a_2}^{c_2} x\right)*V_2 + \left(\sum_{a_3}^{c_3} x\right)*V_3 = SCR_c - SCR_a$$

$$P<S_a,S_e>: \left(\sum_{a_1}^{e_1} v\right)*X_1 + \left(\sum_{a_2}^{e_2} x\right)*V_2 + \left(\sum_{a_3}^{e_3} x\right)*V_3 = SCR_e - SCR_a$$

$$P<S_b,S_c>: \left(\sum_{b_1}^{c_1} v\right)*X_1 + \left(\sum_{b_2}^{c_2} x\right)*V_2 + \left(\sum_{b_3}^{c_3} x\right)*V_3 = SCR_c - SCR_b$$

$$P<S_b,S_e>: \left(\sum_{b_1}^{e_1} v\right)*X_1 + \left(\sum_{b_2}^{e_2} x\right)*V_2 + \left(\sum_{b_3}^{e_3} x\right)*V_3 = SCR_e - SCR_b$$

$$P<S_c,S_e>: \left(\sum_{c_1}^{e_1} v\right)*X_1 + \left(\sum_{c_2}^{e_2} x\right)*V_2 + \left(\sum_{c_3}^{e_3} x\right)*V_3 = SCR_e - SCR_c$$

We can clearly see that the linear independent vectors in the equations' coefficient matrix are $[\sum_{a_1}^{b_1} v, \sum_{a_2}^{b_2} x, \sum_{a_3}^{b_3} x]$, $[\sum_{b_1}^{c_1} v, \sum_{b_2}^{c_2} x, \sum_{b_3}^{c_3} x]$, $[\sum_{c_1}^{e_1} v, \sum_{c_2}^{e_2} x, \sum_{c_3}^{e_3} x]$.

Furthermore, since any three of the four MCSSs intersect in one line, we know that the number of linear independent vectors in the partition plane equations' coefficient matrix is greater than or equal to two.

If the four MCSSs' partition plane equations have only two linear independent vectors, then the planes would intersect in the same line according to the property of linear equations. This is contradictory to the known condition that any three of the four MCSSs intersect in a different line. Hence, the four MCSSs' partition planes' equations have three linear independent vectors.

According to the property of three-variable linear equations, the equation system of the four MCSSs' partition planes has a unique solution. Hence, the four MCSSs intersect at one point.

Lemma 5.3 holds.

Theorem 5.6 *In an n dimension PSS, for i MCSSs where $i \in \{2, 3, \ldots, (n+1)\}$, if any $(i-1)$ of the i MCSSs intersect in a different $(n-i+2)$ dimension space, then the i MCSSs intersect in an $(n-i+1)$ dimension space.*

Proof of Theorem 5.6: Based on the proofs of Lemmas 5.1–5.3, Theorem 5.6 can be proved in the same way.

In the n dimension PSS, the border of two MCSSs is an n-variable linear equation. For a system of n-variable linear equations, if its solution is an m dimension space, then there are $(n - m)$ linear independent vectors in the equation system's coefficient matrix.

Since any $(i - 1)$ of the i MCSSs intersect in an $(n - i + 2)$ dimension space, the $(i - 1)$ MCSSs' equation system has $(i - 2)$ linear independent vectors.

Furthermore, because different $(i-1)$ MCSSs have different $(n-i+2)$ dimension spaces, the i MCSSs' equation system has $(i-1)$ linear independent vectors, which can be proved similarly as Lemma 5.3. Hence, the i MCSSs intersect in an $(n-i+1)$ dimension space.

Theorem 5.6 holds.

Theorem 5.7 *Given DDG segment $\{d_1, d_2, \ldots, d_m\}$ with PSS_1, DDG segment $\{d_{m+1}, d_{m+2}, \ldots, d_n\}$ with PSS_2, and the merged DDG segment $\{d_1, d_2, \ldots, d_m, d_{m+1}, d_{m+2}, \ldots, d_n\}$ with PSS, then we have:*

$$
\forall\, S \in PSS \Rightarrow
\begin{cases}
S = S_1 \cup S_2, \quad S_1 \in PSS_1 \quad S_2 \in PSS_2 \\[2mm]
SCR = SCR_1 + \left(\displaystyle\sum_{k=j+1}^{m} x_k \right) * \left(\displaystyle\sum_{k=m+1}^{i-1} v_k \right) + SCR_2
\end{cases}
$$

where d_j is the last stored data set in the first DDG segment and d_i is the first stored data set in the second DDG segment.

Proof of Theorem 5.7: As stated in Theorem 5.7, in the merged DDG segment under storage strategy S, the regenerations of data sets in DDG segment $\{d_{m+1}, d_{m+2}, \ldots, d_{i-1}\}$ need to start from d_j, which includes the generation cost data sets in DDG segment $\{d_{j+1}, d_{j+2}, \ldots, d_m\}$. Hence,

$$
SCR = SCR_1 + \left(\sum_{k=j+1}^{m} x_k \right) * \left(\sum_{k=m+1}^{i-1} v_k \right) + SCR_2
$$

can be proved by direct utilisation of the definition of SCR, where $(\sum_{k=j+1}^{m} x_k) * (\sum_{k=m+1}^{i-1} v_k)$ is the generation cost rate compensation of data sets in DDG segment $\{d_{j+1}, d_{j+2}, \ldots, d_m\}$ for regenerating data sets in DDG segment $\{d_{m+1}, d_{m+2}, \ldots, d_{i-1}\}$.

Next, we prove

$$
\forall\, S \in PSS \Rightarrow S = S_1 \cup S_2, \quad S_1 \in PSS_1 \quad S_2 \in PSS_2
$$

by apagoge.

We assume $S_1 \notin PSS_1$.

Then we write the total cost rate of the merged DDG segment with MCSSs:

$$
TCR = \sum_{h=1}^{p} (X_h * \sum v_k) + SCR + \sum_{h=1}^{q} (V_h * \sum x_k)
$$

where p and q are the numbers of branches in the merged DDG segment that have preceding data sets and succeeding data sets. Then we have

$$
\begin{aligned}
TCR \;=\; & \sum_{h=1}^{p}\left(X_h * \sum v_k\right) + SCR + \sum_{h=1}^{q}\left(V_h * \sum x_k\right) \\
=\; & \sum_{h=1}^{p}\left(X_h * \sum v_k\right) + SCR_1 + \left(\sum_{k=j+1}^{m} x_k\right) * \left(\sum_{k=m+1}^{i-1} v_k\right) + SCR_2 + \sum_{h=1}^{q}\left(V_h * \sum x_k\right) \\
=\; & \sum_{h=1}^{p_1}\left(X_h * \sum v_k\right) + SCR_1 + \sum_{h=1}^{q_1}\left(V_h * \sum x_k\right) + \left(\sum_{k=j+1}^{m} x_k\right) * \left(\sum_{k=m+1}^{i-1} v_k\right) \\
& + \sum_{h=1}^{p_2}\left(X_h * \sum v_k\right) + SCR_2 + \sum_{h=1}^{q_2}\left(V_h * \sum x_k\right)
\end{aligned}
$$

where p_1 and q_1 are the numbers of branches in the DDG segment $\{d_1, d_2, \ldots, d_m\}$ that have preceding data sets and succeeding data sets except the connecting branch; p_2 and q_2 are the numbers of branches in the DDG segment $\{d_{m+1}, d_{m+2}, \ldots, d_n\}$ that have preceding data sets and succeeding data sets except the connecting branch. Next, we have

$$
TCR = TCR_1 + \sum_{h=1}^{p_2}\left(X_h * \sum v_k\right) + SCR_2 + \sum_{h=1}^{q_2}\left(V_h * \sum x_k\right)
$$

Since $S_1 \notin PSS_1$, given the X values $[X_1, X_2, \ldots, X_{p1}]$, V values $[V_1, V_2, \ldots, V_{q1}]$ and $V = \sum_{k=m+1}^{i-1} v_k$, we can find another MCSS S_1', where $TCR_1' < TCR_1$. Hence, we have

$$
\begin{aligned}
TCR \;=\; & TCR_1 + \sum_{h=1}^{p_2}\left(X_h * \sum v_k\right) + SCR_2 + \sum_{h=1}^{q_2}\left(V_h * \sum x_k\right) \\
>\; & TCR_1' + \sum_{h=1}^{p_2}\left(X_h * \sum v_k\right) + SCR_2 + \sum_{h=1}^{q_2}\left(V_h * \sum x_k\right) \\
=\; & \sum_{h=1}^{p_1}\left(X_h * \sum v_k'\right) + SCR_1' + \sum_{h=1}^{q_1}\left(V_h * \sum x_k'\right) + \left(\sum_{k=j'+1}^{m} x_k\right) * \left(\sum_{k=m+1}^{i-1} v_k\right) \\
& + \sum_{h=1}^{p_2}\left(X_h * \sum v_k\right) + SCR_2 + \sum_{h=1}^{q_2}\left(V_h * \sum x_k\right) \\
=\; & \sum_{h=1}^{p}\left(X_h * \sum v_k'\right) + SCR' + \sum_{h=1}^{q}\left(V_h * \sum x_k\right) = TCR'
\end{aligned}
$$

This is contradictory to the known condition that S is the MCSS of the merged DDG Segment.

Hence, $S_1 \in PSS_1$.

Similarly, we can prove $S_2 \in PSS_2$.

Theorem 5.7 holds.

Lemma 6.1 *The deletion of a stored data set in the* DDG *does not affect the storage status of other stored data sets.*

Proof of Lemma 6.1: Suppose that d_i is a stored data sets to be deleted, d_p is a stored predecessor of d_i and d_f is a stored successor of d_i. If d_i is deleted: (1) more data sets' regenerations need to use d_p, i.e. the deleted successors of d_i; hence, d_p still needs to be stored; (2) the regeneration of d_f needs to start from d_p and regenerate the deleted predecessors of d_i; hence, the generation cost of d_f is increased and d_f still needs to be stored.

Lemma 6.1 holds.

Theorem 6.1 *If a deleted data set is stored, only its adjacent stored predecessors and successors in the* DDG *may need to be deleted to reduce the application cost.*

Proof of Theorem 6.1: Suppose that d_i is a deleted data sets to be stored, d_p is a stored predecessor of d_i and d_f is a stored successor of d_i. If d_i is stored: (1) fewer data sets' regenerations need to use d_p, i.e. regenerations of the deleted successors of d_i can start from d_i; hence, d_p may need to be deleted; (2) the regeneration of d_f can start from d_i instead of d_p; hence, the generation cost of d_f is decreased and d_f may need to be deleted. According to Lemma 6.1, the deletion of d_p and d_f does not affect other stored data sets' storage status.

Theorem 6.1 holds.

Theorem 6.2 *Given a* DDG *and assuming S is the* MCSS *of the* DDG, *if $d_p \in S$ and d_p divides the* DDG *into:*

$$\begin{cases} DDG_1 = \{d_j | d_j \in DDG \wedge d_j \rightarrow d_p\} \\ DDG_2 = \{d_k | d_k \in DDG \wedge d_p \rightarrow d_k\} \end{cases}$$

then S_1 and S_2 are the MCSS*s of* DDG$_1$ *and* DDG$_2$ *respectively, where $S_1 = S \cap DDG_1$ and $S_2 = S \cap DDG_2$.*

Proof of Theorem 6.2: We prove this theorem by apagoge.

1. Suppose there is a storage strategy $S'_1 \neq S_1$ and S'_1 be the MCSS of DDG_1. Then we have:

$$\left(\sum_{d_i \in DDG_1} CostR_i\right)_{S'_1} < \left(\sum_{d_i \in DDG_1} CostR_i\right)_{S_1}$$
$$\Rightarrow \left(\sum_{d_i \in DDG_1} CostR_i\right)_{S'_1} + y_p + \left(\sum_{d_i \in DDG_2} CostR_i\right)_{S_2}$$
$$< \left(\sum_{d_i \in DDG_1} CostR_i\right)_{S_1} + y_p + \left(\sum_{d_i \in DDG_2} CostR_i\right)_{S_2}$$
$$\Rightarrow \left(\sum_{d_i \in DDG_1} CostR_i\right)_{S'_1} + y_p + \left(\sum_{d_i \in DDG_2} CostR_i\right)_{S_2} < \left(\sum_{d_i \in DDG} CostR_i\right)_{S}$$

Then $(\sum_{d_i \in DDG} CostR_i)_{S'} < (\sum_{d_i \in DDG} CostR_i)_S$, $S' = S'_1 \cup \{d_p\} \cup S_2$.

Hence, we get a new storage strategy S' of the DDG which has a smaller cost rate than S. This is contradictory to the known condition 'S is the MCSS of the DDG.' Hence, S_1 is the MCSS of DDG_1.

2. Similarly, it can be proved that S_2 is the MCSS of DDG_2.

Theorem 6.2 holds.

Appendix C
Method of Calculating λ Based on Users' Extra Budget

For designing cost-effective storage strategies, we propose a simple and efficient method to calculate the proper value of λ, with which more data sets can be stored within users' extra budget.

For a given DDG, we can calculate the minimum cost benchmark and further know the storage cost and computation cost in the benchmark, denoted as S and C. Then, we denote the users' extra budget as $\varepsilon\%$, which means users are willing to pay $\varepsilon\%$ more than the benchmark to store the data sets for less data access delay. We further assume in the new strategy that the storage cost is S' and computation cost is C'. Hence in the ideal case, we have

$$(S + C)(1 + \varepsilon\%) = S' + C' \tag{C.1}$$

Due to the $\varepsilon\%$ extra budget, more data sets can be stored; therefore the original minimum cost benchmark is not appropriate for the new strategy. Hence λ is introduced to modify the storage cost in the CTT-SP algorithm, which allows more storage cost in the strategy found by the algorithm. Hence we have the following inequation

$$S'\lambda + C' < S\lambda + C \tag{C.2}$$

In the ideal situation, the computation cost and storage cost should be equal in the trade-off model; therefore we have another equation which is

$$S'\lambda = C' \tag{C.3}$$

Based on Eqs (C.1)–(C.3), we get the following inequation where λ is the only variable

$$S\lambda^2 - (1 + 2\varepsilon\%)(C + S)\lambda + C > 0$$

This inequation has two positive results where λ should be the smaller one.

Based on the above method, we can calculate λ based on users' extra budget. We utilise the method of calculating λ in our strategy which can store more data sets within users' extra budget and reduce the average access time of the data sets.

Bibliography

[1] Amazon Cloud Services. <http://aws.amazon.com/>. Accessed on 3rd December 2012.

[2] Eucalyptus. <http://open.eucalyptus.com/>. Accessed on 3rd December 2012.

[3] Hadoop. <http://hadoop.apache.org/>. Accessed on 3rd December 2012.

[4] Nimbus. <http://www.nimbusproject.org/>. Accessed on 3rd December 2012.

[5] OpenNebula. <http://www.opennebula.org/>. Accessed on 3rd December 2012.

[6] VMware. <http://www.vmware.com/>. Accessed on 3rd December 2012.

[7] Adams I, Long DDE, Miller EL, Pasupathy S, Storer MW. Maximizing efficiency by trading storage for computation. In: Workshop on hot topics in cloud computing. San Diego (CA); 2009. pp. 1−5.

[8] Allcock B, Bester J, Bresnahan J, Chervenak AL, Foster I, Kesselman C, et al. Data management and transfer in high-performance computational grid environments. Parallel Comput 2002;28:749−71.

[9] Alonso G, Reinwald B, Mohan C. Distributed data management in workflow environments. In: Seventh international workshop on research issues in data engineering high performance database management for large-scale applications. Birmingham, UK; 1997. pp. 82−90.

[10] Altintas I, Barney O, Jaeger-Frank E. Provenance collection support in the Kepler scientific workflow system. In: International provenance and annotation workshop. Chicago (IL); 2006. pp. 118−32.

[11] Andrew S, Van Steen M. *Distributed systems: principles and paradigms*. Prentice Hall. Upper Saddle River (NJ); 2007.

[12] Armbrust M, Fox A, Griffith R, Joseph AD, Katz R, Konwinski A, et al. A view of cloud computing. Commun ACM 2010;53:50−8.

[13] Assuncao MDd, Costanzo Ad, Buyya R. Evaluating the cost-benefit of using cloud computing to extend the capacity of clusters. In: 18th ACM international symposium on high performance distributed computing. Garching, Germany; 2009. pp. 141−50.

[14] Bao Z, Cohen-Boulakia S, Davidson SB, Eyal A, Khanna S. Differencing provenance in scientific workflows. In: 25th IEEE international conference on data engineering. Shanghai, China; 2009. pp. 808−19.

[15] Baru C, Moore R, Rajasekar A, Wan M. The SDSC storage resource broker. In: IBM centre for advanced studies conference. Toronto (Ontario, Canada); 1998. pp. 1−12.

[16] Bose R, Frew J. Lineage retrieval for scientific data processing: a survey. ACM Comput Surv 2005;37:1−28.

[17] Brantner M, Florescuy D, Graf D, Kossmann D, Kraska T. Building a database on S3. In: SIGMOD. Vancouver (British Columbia, Canada); 2008. pp. 251−63.

[18] Broberg J, Tari Z. MetaCDN: harnessing 'storage clouds' for high performance content delivery. In: Sixth international conference on service-oriented computing. Sydney, Australia; 2008. pp. 730−1.

[19] Burton A, Treloar, A. Publish my data: a composition of services from ANDS and ARCS. In: Fifth IEEE international conference on e-science. Oxford, UK; 2009. pp. 164−70.

[20] Buyya, R, Venugopal S. The gridbus toolkit for service oriented grid and utility computing: an overview and status report. In: IEEE international workshop on grid economics and business models. Seoul, Korea; 2004. pp. 19–66.

[21] Buyya R, Yeo CS, Venugopal S. Market-oriented cloud computing: vision, hype, and reality for delivering IT services as computing utilities. In: 10th IEEE international conference on high performance computing and communications. Los Alamitos (CA); 2008. pp. 5–13.

[22] Buyya R, Yeo CS, Venugopal S, Broberg J, Brandic I. Cloud computing and emerging IT platforms: vision, hype, and reality for delivering computing as the 5th utility. Future Gener Comput Syst 2009;25:599–616.

[23] Cai M, Chervenak A, Frank M. A peer-to-peer replica location service based on a distributed hash table. In: ACM/IEEE conference on supercomputing. Pittsburgh (PA); 2004.

[24] Chen J, Yang Y. Activity completion duration based checkpoint selection for dynamic verification of temporal constraints in grid workflow systems. Int J High Perform Comput Appl 2008;22:319–29.

[25] Chen J, Yang Y. Temporal dependency based checkpoint selection for dynamic verification of temporal constraints in scientific workflow systems. ACM Trans Softw Eng Methodol 2011;20.

[26] Chervenak A, Deelman E, Foster I, Guy L, Hoschek W, Iamnitchi A, et al. Giggle: a framework for constructing scalable replica location services. In: ACM/IEEE conference on supercomputing. Baltimore (MD); 2002. pp. 1–17.

[27] Chervenak A, Deelman E, Livny M, Su M-H, Schuler R, Bharathi S, et al. Data placement for scientific applications in distributed environments. In: Eighth grid computing conference. Austin (TX); 2007. pp. 267–74.

[28] Chervenak A, Foster I, Kesselman C, Salisbury C, Tuecke S. The data grid: towards an architecture for the distributed management and analysis of large scientific datasets. J Netw Comput Appl 2000;23:187–200.

[29] Chiba T, Kielmann T, Burger Md, Matsuoka S. Dynamic load-balanced multicast for data-intensive applications on clouds. In: IEEE/ACM international symposium on cluster, cloud and grid computing. Melbourne, Australia; 2010. pp. 5–14.

[30] Cho B, Gupta I. New algorithms for planning bulk transfer via internet and shipping networks. In: IEEE 30th international conference on distributed computing systems; 2010. pp. 305–14.

[31] Churches D, Gombas G, Harrison A, Maassen J, Robinson C, Shields M, et al. Programming scientific and distributed workflow with Triana services. Concurrency Comput Pract Exp 2006;18:1021–37.

[32] Dean J, Ghemawat S. MapReduce: simplified data processing on large clusters. Commun ACM 2008;51:107–13.

[33] Deelman E, Blythe J, Gil Y, Kesselman C, Mehta G, Patil S, et al. Pegasus: mapping scientific workflows onto the grid. In: European across grids conference. Nicosia, Cyprus; 2004. pp. 11–20.

[34] Deelman E, Chervenak A. Data management challenges of data-intensive scientific workflows. In: IEEE international symposium on cluster computing and the grid. Lyon, France; 2008. pp. 687–92.

[35] Deelman E, Gannon D, Shields M, Taylor I. Workflows and e-Science: an overview of workflow system features and capabilities. Future Gener Comput Syst 2009;25:528–40.

[36] Deelman E, Singh G, Livny M, Berriman B, Good J. The cost of doing science on the cloud: the montage example. In: ACM/IEEE conference on supercomputing. Austin (TX); 2008. pp. 1–12.

[37] Delic KA, Walker MA. Emergence of the academic computing clouds. ACM Ubiquity 2008;9:1−4.

[38] Dilley J, Maggs B, Parikh J, Prokop H, Sitaraman R, Weihl B. Globally distributed content delivery. IEEE Internet Comput 2002;6:50−8.

[39] Fan X, Cao J, Wu W. Contention-aware data caching in wireless multi-hop ad hoc networks. J Parallel Distrib Comput 2011;71:603−14.

[40] Foster I, Kesselman C. The grid: blueprint for a new computing infrastructure. Morgan Kaufmann. San Francisco (CA); 2004.

[41] Foster I, Vockler J, Wilde M, Yong Z. Chimera: a virtual data system for representing, querying, and automating data derivation. In: 14th international conference on scientific and statistical database management. Edinburgh, Scotland, UK; 2002. pp. 37−46.

[42] Foster I, Yong Z, Raicu I, Lu S. Cloud computing and grid computing 360-degree compared. In: Grid computing environments workshop. Austin (TX); 2008. pp. 1−10.

[43] Garg SK, Buyya R, Siegel HJ. Time and cost trade-off management for scheduling parallel applications on utility grids. Future Gener Comput Syst 2010;26:1344−55.

[44] Glatard T, Montagnat J, Lingrand D, Pennec X. Flexible and efficient workflow deployment of data-intensive applications on grids with MOTEUR. International Journal of High Performance Computing Applications. 2008;22:347−60.

[45] Grossman R, Gu Y. Data mining using high performance data clouds: experimental studies using sector and sphere. In: 14th ACM SIGKDD. Las Vegas (NV); 2008. pp. 920−7.

[46] Grossman RL, Gu Y, Sabala M, Zhang W. Compute and storage clouds using wide area high performance networks. Future Gener Comput Syst 2008;:179−83.

[47] Groth P, Moreau L. Recording process documentation for provenance. IEEE Trans Parallel Distrib Syst 2009;20:1246−59.

[48] Gunda PK, Ravindranath L, Thekkath CA, Yu Y, Zhuang L. Nectar: automatic management of data and computation in datacenters. In: Ninth symposium on operating systems design and implementation. Vancouver (British Columbia, Canada); 2010. pp. 1−14.

[49] Hoffa C, Mehta G, Freeman T, Deelman E, Keahey K, Berriman B, et al. On the use of cloud computing for scientific workflows. In: Fourth IEEE international conference on e-science. Indianapolis (IN); 2008. pp. 640−5.

[50] Huang Y, Cao J, Jin B, Tao X, Lu J, Feng Y. Flexible cache consistency maintenance over wireless ad hoc networks. IEEE Trans Parallel Distrib Syst 2010;21:1150−61.

[51] Jablonski S, Curé O, Rehman M.A, Volz B. DaltOn: an infrastructure for scientific data management. In: Eighth international conference on computational science. Kraków, Poland; 2008. pp. 520−9.

[52] Jia X, Li D, Du H, Cao J. On optimal replication of data object at hierarchical and transparent web proxies. IEEE Trans Parallel Distrib Syst 2005;16:673−85.

[53] Johnston WM, Hanna JRP, Millar RJ. Advances in dataflow programming languages. ACM Comput Surv 2004;36:1−34.

[54] Junwei C, Jarvis SA, Saini S, Nudd GR. GridFlow: workflow management for grid computing. In: Third IEEE/ACM international symposium on cluster computing and the grid. Tokyo, Japan; 2003. pp. 198−205.

[55] Juve G, Deelman E, Vahi K, Mehta G. Data sharing options for scientific workflows on amazon EC2. In: ACM/IEEE conference on supercomputing. New Orleans (LA); 2010. pp. 1−9.

[56] Kondo D, Javadi B, Malecot P, Cappello F, Anderson DP. Cost-benefit analysis of cloud computing versus desktop grids. In: 23rd IEEE international parallel and distributed processing symposium. Rome, Italy; 2009.

[57] Li J, Humphrey M, Agarwal D, Jackson K, Ingen CV, Ryu Y. eScience in the cloud: a MODIS satellite data reprojection and reduction pipeline in the windows azure platform. In: 24th IEEE international parallel and distributed processing symposium. Atlanta (GA); 2010.

[58] Liu DT, Franklin MJ. GridDB: a data-centric overlay for scientific grids. In: 30th VLDB conference. Toronto (Ontario, Canada); 2004. pp. 600−11.

[59] Liu X, Chen J, Yang Y. A probabilistic strategy for setting temporal constraints in scientific workflows. In: Proc. of the sixth international conference on business process management. Milan, Italy; 2008. pp. 180−95.

[60] Liu X, Yuan D, Zhang G, Chen J, Yang Y. SwinDeW-C: a peer-to-peer based cloud workflow system. In: Furht B, Escalante A, editors. Handbook of cloud computing. Springer. New York (NY); 2010. pp. 309−32.

[61] Ludascher B, Altintas I, Berkley C, Higgins D, Jaeger E, Jones M, et al. Scientific workflow management and the Kepler system. Concurrency Comput Pract Exp 2005;1039−65.

[62] Moretti C, Bulosan J, Thain D, Flynn P.J. All-pairs: an abstraction for data-intensive cloud computing. In: 22nd IEEE international parallel and distributed processing symposium. Miami (FL); 2008.

[63] Muniswamy-Reddy K-K, Macko P, Seltzer M. Provenance for the cloud. In: Eighth USENIX conference on file and storage technology. San Jose (CA); 2010. pp. 197−210.

[64] Odifreddi P. Classical recursion theory: the theory of functions and sets of natural numbers. Elsevier. Amsterdam, The Netherlands; 1992. pp. ii−xi, 1−668.

[65] Oinn T, Addis M, Ferris J, Marvin D, Senger M, Greenwood M, et al. Taverna: a tool for the composition and enactment of bioinformatics workflows. Bioinformatics 2004;20:3045−54.

[66] Oram A. Peer-to-peer: harnessing the power of disruptive technologies. SIGMOD Rec 2003;32:57−8.

[67] Osterweil LJ, Clarke LA, Ellison AM, Podorozhny R, Wise A, Boose E, et al. Experience in using a process language to define scientific workflow and generate dataset provenance. In: 16th ACM SIGSOFT international symposium on foundations of software engineering. Atlanta (GA); 2008. pp. 319−29.

[68] Ozsu MT, Valduriez P. Principles of distributed database systems. Upper Saddle River (NJ): Prentice Hall; 1991.

[69] Russell N, ter Hofstede A, Edmond D, van der Aalst W. Workflow data patterns. In: 24th international conference on conceptual modeling. Klagenfurt, Austria; 2005. pp. 353−68.

[70] Simmhan YL, Plale B, Gannon D. A survey of data provenance in e-science. SIGMOD Rec 2005;34:31−6.

[71] Singh G, Vahi K, Ramakrishnan A, Mehta G, Deelman E, Zhao H, et al. Optimizing workflow data footprint. Sci Program 2007;15:249−68.

[72] Stockinger H, Samar A, Holtman K, Allcock B, Foster I, Tierney B. File and object replication in data grids. Cluster Comput 2002;5:305−14.

[73] Stolte E, Praun Cv, Alonso G, Gross T. Scientific data repositories: designing for a moving target. In: ACM SIGMOD international conference on management of data. San Diego (CA); 2003. pp. 349−60.

[74] Szalay AS, Gray J. Science in an exponential world. Nature 2006;440:23−4.

[75] Tatebe O, Morita Y, Matsuoka S, Soda N, Sekiguchi S. Grid datafarm architecture for petascale data intensive computing. In: Second IEEE/ACM international symposium on cluster computing and the. Berlin, Germany; 2002. pp. 102−10.

[76] Thomas GB, Finney RL. Calculus and analytic geometry. 9th ed. Addison-Wesley. Boston (MA); 1995.

[77] Tsakalozos K, Kllapi H, Sitaridi E, Roussopoulos M, Paparas D, Delis A. Flexible use of cloud resources through profit maximization and price discrimination. In: IEEE 27th international conference on data engineering. Hanover, Germany; 2011. pp. 75−86.

[78] Venugopal S, Buyya R, Ramamohanarao K. A taxonomy of data grids for distributed data sharing, management, and processing. ACM Comput Surv 2006;38:1−53.

[79] Venugopal S, Buyya R, Winton L. A grid service broker for scheduling distributed data-oriented applications on global grids. In: Second workshop on middleware in grid computing. Toronto (Ontario, Canada); 2004. pp. 75−80.

[80] Vouk MA. Cloud computing − issues, research and implementations. In: 30th international conference on information technology interfaces. Cavtat, Croatia; 2008. pp. 31−40.

[81] Wang L, Tao J, Kunze M, Castellanos AC, Kramer D, Karl W. Scientific cloud computing: early definition and experience. In: 10th IEEE international conference on high performance computing and communications. Dalin, China; 2008. pp. 825−30.

[82] Warneke D, Kao O. Exploiting dynamic resource allocation for efficient parallel data processing in the cloud. IEEE Trans Parallel Distrib Syst 2011;22:985−97.

[83] Weiss A. Computing in the cloud. ACM Networker 2007;11:18−25.

[84] Wieczorek M, Prodan R, Fahringer T. Scheduling of scientific workflows in the ASKALON grid environment. SIGMOD Rec 2005;34:56−62.

[85] Yang Y, Liu K, Chen J, Lignier J, Jin H. Peer-to-peer based grid workflow runtime environment of SwinDeW-G. In: IEEE international conference on e-science and grid computing. Bangalore, India; 2007. pp. 51−8.

[86] Lee YC, Zomaya AY. Energy conscious scheduling for distributed computing systems under different operating conditions. IEEE Trans Parallel Distrib Syst 2011;22:1374−81.

[87] Yuan D, Yang Y, Liu X, Chen J. A cost-effective strategy for intermediate data storage in scientific cloud workflows. In: 24th IEEE international parallel and distributed processing symposium. Atlanta (GA); 2010.

[88] Yuan D, Yang Y, Liu X, Chen J. A data placement strategy in scientific cloud workflows. Future Gener Comput Syst 2010;26:1200−14.

[89] Yuan D, Yang Y, Liu X, Chen J. A local-optimisation based strategy for cost-effective datasets storage of scientific applications in the cloud. In: Proc. of fourth IEEE international conference on cloud computing. Washington, DC; 2011. pp. 179−186.

[90] Yuan D, Yang Y, Liu X, Chen J. On-demand minimum cost benchmarking for intermediate datasets storage in scientific cloud workflow systems. J. Parallel Distrib Comput 2011;71:316−32.

[91] Yuan D, Yang Y, Liu X, Zhang G, Chen J. A data dependency based strategy for intermediate data storage in scientific cloud workflow systems. Concurrency Comput Pract Exp 2012;24:956−76.

[92] Zaharia M, Konwinski A, Joseph AD, Katz R, Stoica I. Improving MapReduce performance in heterogeneous environments. In: Eighth USENIX symposium on operating systems design and implementation. San Diego (CA); 2008. pp. 29−42.

Printed and bound by CPI Group (UK) Ltd, Croydon, CR0 4YY

03/10/2024

01040426-0012